The Emotional Maintenance Manual

Also by Nathaniel Lande:

Mindstyles/Lifestyles
Stages

The Emotional Maintenance Manual

Nathaniel Lande

Rawson, Wade Publishers, Inc. · New York

The author wishes to thank Price, Stern & Sloane for permission to reprint a selection fom *A Winner's Notebook*
by Theodore Rubin.

Library of Congress Cataloging in Publication Data

Lande, Nathaniel.
   The emotional maintenance manual.

   Bibliography: p.
   Includes index.
   1. Depression, Mental. I. Title.
RC537.L34   1979   616.8'52   78-64799
ISBN 0-89256-088-6
ISBN 0-89256-098-3 pbk.

Published simultaneously in Canada
by McClelland and Stewart, Ltd.
Manufactured in the United States of America
Composition by American Book-Stratford Press,
Brattleboro, Vermont
Printed and bound by R. R. Donnelly & Sons Company,
   Crawfordsville, Indiana
Designed by Gene Siegel
First Edition

FOR ANDREW

Acknowledgments

The making of a book comes from a lifetime of thought and experience. There are many who are responsible.

Grateful acknowledgment is made to:

Dr. Jessie Marmorston, friend and advisor, for her careful and fine introduction.

Susan Buchanan M.A., whose spirit and quiet insight fills these pages.

Dr. David Glass of UCLA.

Dr. George Serban, New York University.

Dr. Harvey Mindess, Antioch College.

Dr. Al Erdynast, Antioch College.

Dr. Melanie Allen, Antioch College.

Dr. Robert Greenblatt, Medical College of Georgia.

Dr. William Bunney, National Institute of Health.

Dr. Hans Selye, Institute of Experimental Medicine, University of Montreal.

Dr. Virginia Sukoff.

Dr. John Lilly.

Dr. Ernest Lykissas.

All doctors whose concern and compassion for the healing arts have taught me more than I know.

Three researchers who have diligently developed this program with me and who are doctoral candidates at UCLA:
Douglas Smith
George Maldonado
Kam Booi Hon
Thank you. I am indebted to your brilliance.

And to Afton Slade who graciously gave thought to the early concepts and whose contribution on cycles and emotional maintenance is acknowledged and sincerely appreciated.

To Roslyn Targ whose support and friendship encouraged this manuscript, to Sharon Morgan and Sandi Gelles-Cole, my editors, Eleanor and Kennett Rawson, my publishers, Nancy Moss, Cathrine Mellquist, Lawrence Lande, Barbara Metzler, Dennis Metzler, Shiela Lane Reed, Jean Sully, Paige Rense, Elliot Rose, Marge Levee, Byron Clark, Hal Weiser, Larry Sloan, and Andrew Lande, all of whom in different ways have enriched the quality of my life.

To Shirley-Lee Kam, whose organization of material for the author was superb.

I am grateful to Mark Stern and Hazel Rae, of the National Institute of Health, who have opened doors to great thoughts and helped me so much during the writing of this book.

Nathaniel Lande
Beverly Hills, California, 1979

Contents

Introduction

In my long career as an endocrinologist and professor of clinical medicine at the University of Southern California, I have spent a lifetime studying physical and mental health. From time to time I am asked to evaluate articles and books related to emotional and physical well-being. Nathaniel Lande has been my friend and student for many years and I consider it a great honor to be part of his work. *The Emotional Maintenance Manual* is outstanding. In writing *The Emotional Maintenance Manual*, Nathaniel Lande has succeeded where many of the best scientific researchers and psychotherapists have failed. He has brought recently discovered, revolutionary concepts of mental health out of the research laboratory where they were born, and applied them to everyday life, where they belong. He has taken these new findings, integrated them with the best and most established techniques for treating mental distress, and depression and created a total program for assuring emotional health. This book is a breakthrough in self-help psychotherapy.

In my work I have studied stress and developed a code

of behavior for understanding and dealing with it. My primary interest has been in the field of experimental medicine and its application to endocrinology: the relationship of biochemistry and the human situation.

Here Lande has identified a multidimensional approach for the healthy person; an active program for fine-tuning you psychologically, and for keeping you fit for life. It is a mindbody concept integrating the many variables that influence emotions and behavior.

The workings of the human mind, the mechanisms and reasons behind the great majority of human feelings and behavior, are still sometimes elusive and mysterious. We know there are many variables that all interact together in a complex manner to determine how you feel and behave in any given situation. Such factors as nutrition, biochemistry, exercise, genetic traits, stress, life change, life experience, belief systems, the cycles and rhythms of the body, learned behavior, disease, emotions, and environmental variables all can affect your psychological well-being. Of course, there is no *one* cause for mental distress. The chances are that there is a need for a psychological maintenance program because of the complex interaction of many of the possible causes mentioned above.

Indeed, cases where clients have spent many years and thousands of dollars going from therapist to therapist, searching for the cause and solution to their problems are not uncommon. The sad truth is that many therapists deal with only one or two of the causes that might possibly be the root of their client's psychological illness. The factors that affect the way we feel and act are so complexly interrelated that a therapy dealing with only one or a few of the possible causes of emotional distress simply can not work for everyone, all the time. There can be many holistic solutions.

Emotional fitness results from a balanced biochemistry, proper exercise and diet, and clear thinking. *The Emotional Maintenance Manual* is designed to deal with all the variables that have been found to influence the way we act and feel.

The program recognizes and puts into practice recent scientific discoveries about the interrelationship of the mind and body. Scientific studies continually indicate the many complex ways in which mind and body interact. What we believe can have powerful effects on our bodies. For example, patients with chronic pain, when given a placebo and told the pills are new, powerful painkillers, many times report a welcome relief from the ever-constant pain. And physical changes can have powerful effects on the way we feel. A diet and exercise regimen can affect our emotions by altering our biochemistry.

Even more revolutionary are the discoveries that our moods are affected by changes in the amount of chemical substances in the brain called neurotransmitters. Studies done on people that have committed suicide have determined that there is a significant difference in the amount of certain of these neurotransmitters in their brains as compared to people who have died by accident or natural causes.

But most revolutionary of all are those studies indicating that you can restore your neurotransmitters to their normal balance, and regain your emotional health, by a regular program of exercise, a well-planned diet, proper oxygenation, and a multidimensional approach to therapy. The EMM shows you how to make these exciting breakthroughs work for you, to help you feel better than you ever have before, and to keep you feeling this good throughout life.

This book is the start of a revolution in the treatment of mental distress in that it is a *preventive* approach to mental well-being. It has been my experience as a physician, and a human being, that the best time to deal with a problem is before it becomes one. In my years as a physician I've seen patients who have ignored treatable body infections for so long that by the time they came to me for treatment, permanent damage had left them scarred for life. Physical and emotional problems are best treated at an early stage when you are still healthy, before they become patterned behaviors with irreversible effects. The EMM is a continuing maintenance program, which teaches you how to achieve psychological well-being and gives you the tools and prescriptions for problem solving.

I recommend the EMM as an excellent guide for the maintenance of psychological fitness. The 3-day Crash Program and the 8-Point Tune-up is not only a workable concept but also a valuable reference source, for it is a distillation of revolutionary scientific breakthroughs. It takes a sound concept from the best and the most proven psychotherapies. It is designed and proven to work. To work in all those willing to give up what they are for what they could become.

Jessie Marmorston, M.D., F.A.C.P.

Editor's Note:

Dr. Marmorston is Clinical Professor of Medicine at the University of Southern California School of Medicine. Formerly she was Professor of Experimental Medicine at USC.

She is currently principal Investigator for the Multiple Risk Factor Intervention Trial, a 20-clinic, nationwide study. She has received 36 international awards which include:

Ciba Foundation Award,
Phi Sigma Sigma "Woman of the Year" Award,
Salerni Collegium Award of Merit,
Los Angeles Times "Woman of the Year" Award,
Reiss-Davis Clinic for Child Guidance, Golden Key Foundation "Community Service Award,"
Willard O. Thompson Award, American Geriatrics Society,
The Lasker Award for Research In Endocrinology.

Dr. Marmorston has written 150 scientific articles and 4 books. Among them are.

Psychoanalysis and the Human Condition,
Internal Resistance and Clinical Medicine,
Midas: Medical Information Data Analysis System.

PART I

The EMM

THE EMM ROADMAP

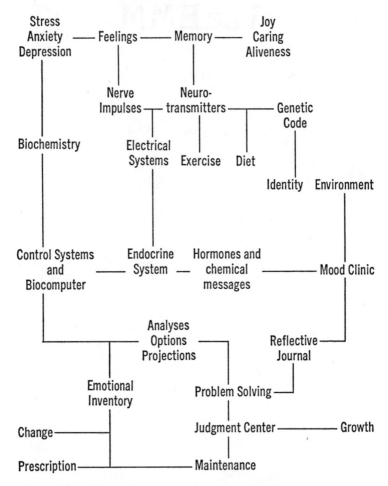

You are about to embark on a journey through sometimes familiar, often unfamiliar, territory. The signs and guideposts in the roadmap offer an overview of the entire trip from starting point to final destination. As you read the book, you will begin to understand the interrelationships between the pathways. They cross, bisect, and intersect, but they are all necessary stops along the road to emotional well-being.

Charting
the Course

This book is an intersection in your life. At the crossroads of depression and happiness you can choose which road to take.

The concept is for the healthy person.

A bold statement: If you are an average individual and in reasonably good health, as most of us are, you need not "fight depression" again. But you will have to give up three days of your life and be part of the preventative maintenance program to realize your full potential.

You will learn new behavior and change old thoughts.

I know the warning signs and the feelings and the symptoms. I have seen the program work extraordinarily well. I know it will work for you, too.

But what about this? How did this program come about, and why?

In the spring of 1974, I read a psychology text by a colleague, Ken Dallet. That's what its official designation was; to me, it was poetry, philosophy. It was keenly intelligent and profoundly moving. I wrote to Dr. Dallet some months later, at the University of California, where he taught. The letter was returned. I phoned in order to track him down, and I found that he had taken his own life.

Why? A man so sensitively informed about the vicissitudes of human nature, so much better equipped, one would think, to deal with his personal problems than most of us are.

Why? The question haunts us. A seventeen-year-old honor student, class president, football hero; a young TV star rocketed from oblivion to fame in a couple of years; the housewife down the street with a loving husband, three healthy children, dogs, cats, a maid, pool, trim figure and pretty face, friends, vacations, and a new car. Why?

What sort of secret turmoil could provoke such a tragic and final action? Was it their inability to cope with this fast-paced, tough, impersonal, competitive world? But these people were outwardly the most successful of their peers. What went wrong?

Of the three to four million people who try to take their own lives each year, 365,000 are successful. And although there are 25–30,000 reported suicides in the United States each year—one every twenty minutes—authorities believe the actual number is much larger. Using just the reported figure, suicide is the tenth leading cause of adult death in the country; the third among people aged fifteen to nineteen. In a National Institute of Health study of 264 suicides made by Dr. Warren Breen of Tulane University, the typical suicide feels that "his goals are unreached, his friends are distancing, his self-conception hits bottom." Dr. Norman Farberow, co-founder of the pioneer Los Angeles Suicide Prevention Center, lists some of the chief characteristics of potential suicides: they are depressed and unhappy, with feelings of worthlessness, hopelessness, helplessness. Anger, hostility, rejection are also characteristics, as are feelings of inadequacy, incapability, unlovability.

Depression is the most common psychological problem we face, and the most difficult to solve. What is it? Some psychologists have described it as learned helplessness. Others define depression as a reduction in activity that takes place when an important reinforcement in the individual's environment is taken away. This can become a vicious circle—after the reduction of activity, the depressive behavior may itself be reinforced by sympathy or solicitous attention from others and situations that will reinforce positive activity become even less available as a result of inactivity. When you add to depression other emotional ailments—anxiety alienation, obsessive and compulsive thinking and behavior, alcohol and drug abuse—you realize that you are talking about a large portion of the population!

What causes these problems, so widespread and so chronic? Why do we consume millions of tranquilizers annually, run to psychiatrists, counsellors, astrologers, join groups, take weekend head trips? The answers are as numerous as the problems. An unhappy childhood or an inherited parental tendency towards worry; a diet of junk food and sedentary habits; possibly hypoglycemia or low blood sugar, which can be a cause of depression, insomnia, anxiety. And the normal traumas of life leave the temporary or permanent psychological damage in their wake—a broken relationship; economic failure; the financial, social, and emotional vicissitudes that affect us all. Most depression is triggered by such life stresses; unfortunately it doesn't always disappear even when the stress recedes. And there are anxieties and depressions which seem to erupt spontaneously, with no apparent cause, yet which produce psychic pain as acute as that following a traumatic event.

If the masonry of our society is cracking, then our tremendous rate of change has widened the fissures all through the structure. Families are fragmented, there is less authority in religious, social, and moral institutions. We yearn for a secure place in a firm network of social and personal relationships.

What can we do about it? There are psychotherapists of a hundred disciplines, psychics, mind control courses, meditation classes, hot tubs, cold baths, martinis, cruises to the West

Indies—everything and anything has been prescribed to lift us out of the blue-black depths, make us more effective and bring us happiness.

Two hundred fifty million prescriptions are filled in the United States every year. Over $1 billion a year is spent on one major tranquilizer—Valium. Sixty percent of all hospital beds are occupied by people suffering from mental illness. Twenty-six percent of our population suffers from depression acute enough to require treatment. Ninety-five percent of psychiatric therapy and psychological counseling deals with symptoms of depression.

All of these people are silently shouting for help. Why, given that superbly designed instrument, the human mind/body, did they abdicate responsibility for it, stop caring for it? That question was one I felt compelled to answer; to search and develop, with my colleagues, a system for preventive mental maintenance.

My colleagues and I began our work with a basic premise: we are the product of our genetic code, our biochemistry, and our environment. These three factors influence our lives at different times, in different relationships, at different perspectives. Genetics, physiology, nutrition, learning, fluctuations in rhythms and cycles, and cognitive influences all play a part in shaping us. Too many therapists are sold on their own research specialties, and come to think that their own way of looking at behavior has all the answers. Research to date just doesn't support that kind of thinking. Until research has isolated causes for behavior, we felt that the most successful therapy should include all possible approaches. After all, the goal of psychological treatment is to bring about behavior change, not to support a theory. We also felt the need to structure a total program to teach patterns of problem solving, and not just ways to deal with one specific problem. Psychology is in a constant state of flux and there is little scientific data to support the many mindstyles in the marketplace today, so we analyzed and distilled over seventy psychoanalytical schools—

Freud, Sullivan, Jung, Adler, Horney, Maslow, Gestalt, Transactional Analysis, Behavior Modification, Crisis Intervention, Family Therapy.

These are just some of the many therapies popular today. In many instances treatment can help you deal with life crises and the emotional and behavioral problems that interfere significantly with the conduct of life. But we could find no preventive mental health approach focusing upon the intrinsic complexity of the individual and the richness of his mind. We wanted a program the individual could utilize to remain healthy and minimize the need for any future professional help.

We also knew that most people seeking help for emotional illness ask their doctor, a minister, or a friend who has received therapy. It is often difficult to weed out the charlatans, and those who promise more than they can deliver. Dr. Lewis Paul of Los Angeles warns against the recent increase in superstition, the belief in the occult, and advocates a healthy skepticism. There is a great risk of quasi-religious cults, novel psychotherapies, wisdom schools such as Arica, est, encounter groups, all of which tend to rely on enthusiasm alone rather than the hard work of self-examination needed for real change.

We looked for a fresh approach to psychotherapy, for we believe in man's built-in capacity for growth and self-actualization. We looked into philosophy and lastly turned to science and the medical profession, and in this process we found the genesis of what we were looking for.

During a recent seminar at the College of William and Mary in Williamsburg, Virginia, sponsored by the National Institute of Mental Health, some of the world's leading physicians, neurologists, and neuroendocrinologists discussed some rather startling findings concerning the role of physiological processes in depressive states. The results were a product of years of investigation by researchers from all over the country. New information was reported on the action of neurotransmitter substances in the brain and their relationship to activity and depression. The discovery of these transmitting substances, called amines, represents the first breakthrough in the search for the biochemical causes of depression, and as a result, there now appears to be a direct link between the biogenic amines and depressive illness.

Two substances, which you yourself can manufacture, actually fight depression and monitor stress. They are norepinephrine and serotonin. In very simple terms, the adrenal glands, activated by environmental stress or exercise, determine the amount of adrenaline in your body. Adrenaline serves as a precursor to the neurotransmitters and neurohormones norepinephrine and serotonin. These chemicals are manufactured by the brain to facilitate the transmission of nerve impulses throughout the body. Studies have shown that people deficient in norepinephrine are more likely to be tired, listless, and depressed. In addition, it is the serotonin mechanism that controls the flow of oxygen in your blood.

But perhaps the most interesting discovery about these chemicals is that you can control their production through diet and exercise. Certain foods and exercise actually stimulate their production.

As a result of these extraordinary findings, we developed a comprehensive program that was unique and revolutionary. It was important to our staff to develop a mood clinic, a 3-day crash program, and a lifelong maintenance program—built on scientific fact and research—so that each individual could improve the quality of his or her life. It was a concept tailored and fashioned for each individual, one that he or she could be a part of. A multidimensional approach to behavior that combined diet with physical exercise and psychological discipline. We wanted an interaction of mind and body—of emotion and biochemistry. We felt that this new approach could help recognize the patterns of life and enable one to detect the early signs of emotional problems. The plan of action was designed so the individual could maintain emotional balance. After three years of research, we tested the concept.

From January 1978 to August 1978, 118 people took part in a research program designed to test the effectiveness of the Emotional Maintenance 3-Day Crash Program and the Lifelong Maintenance Program. The results were outstanding.

The 118 subjects were a diverse group, ethnically, geographically, and socially. Their ages ranged from 20 to 48. There were professors, cab drivers, doctors, lawyers, writers, secretaries, housewives, a psychiatrist, a sports car driver, a professional athlete, actors, actresses, medical students, newspaper reporters, college students, airline stewardesses, businessmen, blue-collar workers as well as white-collar workers, and several that were unemployed. Seventy percent of the participants came from Antioch College, the University of California at Los Angeles, and the surrounding Los Angeles area. Twenty percent of the subjects were from the East Coast. And 5 percent were foreigners from Canada, Mexico, France, Germany, and England.

Their reasons for volunteering to participate in this study were many. Many of the subjects were having problems coping with the crises and stresses of life; depression, anxiety, phobias, loss of control, feelings of helplessness and meaninglessness of life, insomnia, constant fatigue, inability to cope with divorce, mid-life crises, identity crises, inability to recover from the loss of a relationship, problems at work and at home. Approximately one-third of our subjects had at one time in their life been involved in psychotherapy. Approximately one-third had been involved in other forms of self-improvement such as TM, est, yoga, and Zen. And approximately one-third of our subjects had never in their lives felt the need for psychotherapy or any self-help regimen—they felt good about themselves, but were open to the idea of maximizing their potential in life.

At the end of four days and again at the end of six months, the subjects took the same emotional inventory they had taken at the beginning of the program along with a set of tests and controls we had devised to measure emotional change. Most of the participants developed a fuller understanding of their emotions and became more aware of their own needs, patterns, and motivations as well as the perspectives and points of view of the people around them. They learned how to prevent major depression before it started and how to realize their goals: what to do; how to take charge of their lives; how to feel better and happier and look at life more realistically. The results were impressive. The program had winning qualities. We knew it worked and now we want to share the program with you.

Can it work for you? Yes.

We all go through periods in our lives when we question our beliefs, the expectations we hold for ourselves, the relationships we have with others, and the types of experience we need for personal growth. But to embark on the EMM program you must be willing to move from familiar territory, to discover new vistas; to change and to grow. It is work, and not always easy. But it is rich in dividends. By the time you finish the program you will shift old thought patterns, change the focus of your life, and remodel your emotional make-up for a fuller and happier life.

Few of us give attention to the maintenance of our emotional health. Usually we seek help only after an alarming knock has developed or our machinery seriously malfunctions; red or yellow warning lights flash in our consciousness but we take a tranquilizer, pour a drink, turn on the television, ignore or repress the danger signals.

The Emotional Maintenance Manual offers a preventive, continuing maintenance program; a program designed to teach you how to deal with small problems before they become overwhelming or dangerous. The Manual will help you chart your present condition and indicate specific steps to correct future mood swings.

Like most of us, your state of mind probably hovers in a range between extremes. The difference between being up or down is knowing how to use abilities you already possess. This complete, detailed program will provide techniques to help you use those abilities to conquer your fears, your feelings of insecurity and inferiority, of rage and resentment, until you reach the point where you can live with yourself and like it. By learning to channel thoughts, words, actions, you take control of your emotions, shape your life, make your world what you want it to be.

To make this program work, you must put your emotional health ahead of everything else in your life and take full responsibility for your state of mind. According to psychotherapist Dr. Phillip Oderberg, "people tend to be passive, following the physical principle of inertia." Our society tends to foster passivity. That's part of our problem today. People want to be happy, yet they are unwilling to give in terms of energy, libido, and time to make the changes necessary to achieve real happiness. As Abraham Lincoln said, "most people are about as happy as they make up their minds to be."

So get up off the couch, write yourself a new script, and prepare yourself for action. You're the only one who can bring about change in yourself. The EMM is a guide to show you exactly how you *can* change and in the process create changes in everything around you. Your happiness, your peace of mind, your attitudes, the way you look and feel and talk are in your hands. It's up to you to act instead of reacting!

The EMM is divided into four sections: first, an introduction. Second, the Emotional Maintenance Inventory, set up to test your present state of mind, and the uniquely designed 3-Day Crash Program, a multifaceted system wherein the primary purpose is to head you in a new direction. Third is the Lifelong Maintenance Program, the outline of a regimen that you adjust to your individual needs and follow, as its name would suggest, for life. Fourth is a manual for maximum performance, an in-depth study of various aspects of emotional well-being—good nutrition, exercise, creativity—and tune-up areas.

Your first step, then, is to take the Emotional Maintenance Inventory, and embark on the 3-Day Crash Program after a short preparation. Follow up with the Lifelong Maintenance Program. In both areas, specific and special cognitive process exercises have been included to prevent possible malfunctions before they occur. Then read the chapters on specific problem areas, with specially devised "prescriptions" to administer when you need them. Remember, the EMM is not a book you are going to read and put on your bookshelf; it is a *manual* for living that you will use for a long, long time.

Emotions give color to our experience. The kind and degree of emotions we have as individuals define our personalities to others. Emotions are counterpoints to our motives and rational behavior. Feelings of sadness and ecstasy, excitement and fear, give life its special quality.

Each of us has experienced anxiety and depression. They are completely normal reactions and, kept within bounds, serve a positive function in our environment. Yet the 1970s were characterized early in the decade as the Age of Anxiety and then as the Age of Depression. Does this mean our coping mechanisms have blown a fuse? Are we subjected to so much stress that our emotions have run rampant?

This recognition of the immobilizing aspects of anxiety and depression is evident in the abundance of self-help books that have entered the market in recent years. There are books designed to make their readers happy, confident, powerful; teach them to overcome feelings of inferiority; straighten out their sagging psyches and knotted personal relationships—in short, to chart a thousand and one better ways to be.

The books don't always work. We read them, make a few resolutions, try some of the approaches, sharpen our thinking for a few days, and dutifully repeat the affirmations and formulas. We then lapse back into the same old patterns of living until the next trumpet call is heard proclaiming the arrival of a new method of coping, another blueprint for traveling unscathed through the difficulties of living.

The Emotional Maintenance Manual operates under a different set of assumptions. Emotions, collectively, are the barometer of our well-being, and we must understand them. For example, negative emotions indicating anxiety and depression can be useful expressions which lead to the development of rich and fulfilling lives. The ability to express emotions, both positive and negative ones, and make them work for you, is an important asset.

The Emotional Maintenance Manual was conceived as a guide to help you look after yourself, to keep your mind and body in good working order, fight depression and increase your neurotransmitter activity. It is meant to be kept on your nighttable to consult at a moment's notice, just as you keep your car's manual in the glove compartment. It is structured to help you pay attention to and interpret warning signs when they occur. It is, however, a maintenance manual, not a repair manual; if you are badly run down, you need professional help immediately!

Throughout these pages, you will learn how to respect and take charge of your emotional biocomputer—that part of you, mental, spiritual, and physical, that makes you *feel*. *The Emotional Maintenance Manual* is designed for maximum performance. It is the ultimate self-help book. Through the 3-Day Crash Program, it demands action *now* and gives you a chance to experience immediate results. But if you wish to lead a life free of debilitating, energy-sapping emotional ups and downs that you don't understand and can't control, the Manual demands that you be able to give up what you are for what you could become.

Again, I want to emphasize that the approach of the EMM is a multidimensional one, in keeping with recent attitudes in psychotherapy. The three keystones of emotional maintenance are mental conditioning, exercise, and diet. In the 3-Day Crash Program you will find exercises for the body, for visual and emotional imagination, for memory, for relaxation, for digestion; exercises that probe, that make you feel, that demand that you change course *right now!* The diversity of these exercises reflects the emphasis on modern psychological theory on man's built-in capacity of growth and self-actualization.

The EMM utilizes a biochemical approach built upon a number of philosophies, disciplines, and therapeutic concepts. It is based primarily on two such concepts. The first, insight therapy, assumes that problem behavior occurs because the subject doesn't understand his underlying motivation and will be healed when he does. The second, behavior-modification therapy, aims to change abnormal and/or undesirable patterns by using various conditioning and desensitization processes. The main process among the latter is cognition, or *knowing:* running yourself through a situation before it happens so that you gain practice in performing acceptably when it actually does happen.

But much of the material in the book—relating mainly to diet and physical exercise—is based on breakthrough mind-body approaches to medicine and biochemical research discussed in the next chapter. Through the diet and exercises outlined in the EMM crash program and explained fully in later chapters, you will learn to modify and even control your body's production of mood- and energy-affecting hormones, thereby increasing your tolerance for the stressful situations that surround us every day.

Collecting research and devising and testing exercises for the EMM has been an enormous project; outstanding physicians, endocrinologists, neurobiologists, psychologists, nutritionists, and physical education experts have contributed to and supervised the preparation of various parts of the manuscript.

You will find case studies, charts, and test results on those subjects and faculty who have reviewed the EMM and have taken its 3-Day Crash Program, in the Appendix.

The Emotional Maintenance Program has been researched, driven, and tested. It works. Guide yourself through it and you will feel better than you have ever felt in your life.

THE EMOTIONAL WHEEL

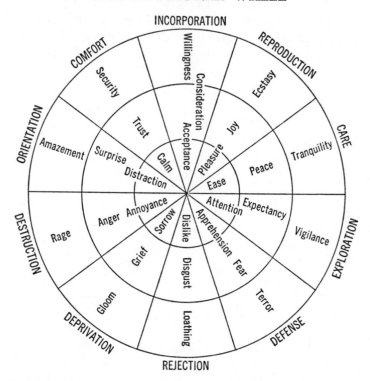

Emotions are barometers of feelings; counterpoints to our motives and behavior. In 1880, William James assumed that bodily changes such as rapid breathing and perspiration were directly stimulated by fear. Emotion, he reported, is nothing more than our awareness of bodily changes as they take place. Since James' initial theories, there has been subsequent investigation of the hypothesis that emotions themselves determine bodily changes and vice versa.

On the emotional wheel, emotions are organized by similarity, intensity, and polarity. Emotions next to each other in the circle are far apart. In fact, emotions that are opposites in the circle are opposites in life. Within the circle, the farther an emotion is toward the edge, the more intense it is. Thus, rage is more intense an emotion than anger, which is more intense than annoyance. This circle helps us to understand the meaning and degree of our emotionality.

Take the Wheel

There are times when we must change the course of our lives, moving outside the comfortable, knowable control of our personal cycles, because the new road, though frightening at first and unfamiliar, will get us where we want to go, and get us there faster, with fewer detours.

This is the sort of change that the EMM is going to ask you to demand of yourself. I know it's not easy—it requires will power, discipline, and intelligence. I think a few words on the nature of change will help you prepare yourself.

The most difficult part of any program for change is getting started. We have to keep reminding ourselves that all behavior is learned and can be unlearned. In experiments with dogs artificially conditioned by repeated shocks they couldn't avoid, the animals eventually gave up any attempt to resist and settled into apathy.

We react similarly: if your repeated attempts to achieve something—a good, lasting relationship, job promotion—are punished with failure and not rewarded with success, you eventually stop trying, and you pretend to yourself that "it wasn't really all that important," or "there are other things in life." When conditions were altered so that crossing a wooden barrier would make it possible for the dogs to avoid the shocks, it was necessary to actually drag them across the barrier many times before they finally learned the avoidance procedure on their own. When they made the discovery that there was something they could do to help themselves, their recovery was complete and permanent.

Again the situation is analogous: if you finally realize that you could get your promotion by making a horizontal move in your corporation first, or if a good friend points out to you that you almost always date girls who are unable to make a commitment in this liberated age, then suddenly that promotion and the hope of finding that someone would become important, and you would start trying again.

Two of the main objectives of the 3-Day Crash Program are to teach you the mechanics of change—how to go about changing, what it feels like, how to keep at it; and to engage you in your first acts of self-willed, directed change.

Constructive thinking is the impetus, positive action is the answer. Hamlet wondered "whether to take arms against a sea of troubles, and by opposing, end them," but agonized endlessly over taking any action at all. In Merle Miller's book *Plain Speaking*, he quotes Harry Truman as saying, "I don't think knowing what's the right thing to do ever gives anybody too much trouble. It's *doing* the right thing that seems to give a lot of people trouble."

Automotive technicians recommend against coasting very far with the engine off or towing a vehicle for a long distance. Even with gears in neutral the transmission is properly lubricated only when the engine is running; and you have far less control of your car. It works the same way in your life. You risk serious emotional injury if you let yourself drift or be towed. You must know what you're doing, take command, be in charge. The feeling of helplessness is one of the major causes of depression, anxiety, stress. People deprived of opportunities during childhood development to control their own rewards and punishments become intensely vulnerable to states of depression, helplessness, apathy.

We're creatures of habit in both mind and body—when we try to change, everything in us resists. When we have been shocked into apathy or learned helplessness, like the dogs in the experiment, our attitudes and actions fix themselves in grooves. When those habitual defeatist attitudes recur, we have to shut them off instantly and replace them with brighter, newer ideas. But marshalling a whole regiment of determined positive thoughts will accomplish nothing as long as you, the commander, lie there and languish. You have to act!

People who are accustomed to controlling the course of their own lives usually see the future optimistically. You have to learn a wide repertoire of coping techniques and responses to use in every type of situation: then you are armed and ready for the battle. And you must keep trying new tasks, take stances of increasing difficulty. Each time you succeed, tackle something more difficult.

Determine to affect your environment instead of reflecting it. Don't sit back and echo the ideas of others, mirror their opinions. Speak with your own voice, make your own vibrations. You can radiate depression—people can sense it when you walk into a room, even though you may be smiling—or you can radiate vitality, competence, control.

Confront your fears head on; every day do at least one thing that frightens you. Each time it gets easier. If you're a coward, pretend to be a tiger; the familiar admonition to behave "as if" can work wonders. A much-decorated French general, admired by his troops as totally fearless, confessed to a friend that in reality he was filled with fears but he made his body move steadily forward, doing the things that terrified him, pretending not even to notice the dangers, until it became automatic.

Psychological stress is a way of life in our high-pressure, competitive, fractured society; conflicting pulls create physical and psychological disturbances. Rats tested in an environment in which shock was administered whenever they approached food or water were in severe conflict over whether to try for the food or avoid the shock. After two weeks many developed ulcers; some died from hemorrhages. There are similar conflicts in human society; particularly in men the need for comfort and affection stands in opposition to social demands to be strong, independent, aggressive. Men are still required to be the bulwark of the family, yet the increasing independence of women and their competition in the work environment gives men less emotional support than they received in the past. Women have greater freedom to take on new roles, yet these very opportunities are creating stress for many women. With such a wide range of choices, decisions become difficult. Dr. Hans Selye, world-famous endocrinologist and leading expert on stress, has said he knows of no single situation that is more damaging, more stressful, than being faced with a number of alternatives and forced to choose amongst them, without any solid criteria upon which to base the decision. In addition, women are still a little unsure, a bit defensive, in formerly masculine occupations. They feel they must be twice as competent as men, and are subjected to putdowns and resentment from traditionally-minded chauvinists.

Essential hypertension, a disorder characterized by chronic high blood pressure that has no apparent cause, is apparently related to various stressful conditions, traumatic events, anger, anxiety. Subjects who lost their jobs were studied over many months and were found to have higher blood pressure both in anticipation of their dismissal and after they were fired than a control group in similar occupations who were still employed. Other studies indicate that blood pressure can be elevated by feelings of helplessness and repressing aggressive impulses. Aggression against a source of frustration helps lower blood pressure.

Some of our neurotic anxieties are acquired in childhood when we are punished for impulsive acts. We then develop a generalized fear of disastrous consequences that could follow upon taking any decisive, aggressive action. A significant amount of such conditioning induces apathy, helplessness, a loss of spontaneity in our daily living, and creates timidity and self-consciousness.

Many experts have researched and studied the ramifications of controlling one's life; or more importantly, *believing* that you are in control, which has an equally salubrious effect. Bruno Bettelheim, the world-famous child psychologist and essayist, has written about the reaction of prisoners to conditions in Nazi concentration camps. Those who came to believe that they would never leave the camp except as corpses, who were convinced they could exercise no influence whatsoever over their destiny, were, in a sense, walking corpses. Deprived of self-esteem and every form of stimulation, emotionally and physically exhausted, the camp environment had total power over them. Those prisoners who clung to hope, who believed they still had a future, often did survive and in a relatively undamaged emotional state.

Experiments with sheep repeatedly given mild shocks they couldn't control caused them to scream, defecate, jump about wildly; their helplessness in the face of this relatively mild trauma appeared responsible for their behavioral breakdown.

Physiologist Walter Cannon made a study of voodoo deaths and reported they really do occur. The individual, through pervasive social conditioning, who believes he is doomed, cannot control his fear of what he regards as all-powerful forces working to destroy him; he meekly surrenders to his fate and dies.

Researcher and distinguished physician E. Mandler says the feeling of not being in control is a central characteristic of neurotic anxiety.

We all have periods when we feel weak, inadequate, full of error. We're not satisfied with ourselves as we are—we want to be different, really different. With the right conditioning in confidence, in faith in ourselves, and with action, we can make our personal universes more to our liking.

In the following chapters you will learn to construct some new patterns of positive thinking, work on your self-esteem, gather all information relevant to your life and your problems and think about them in creative ways. Then, you'll take action to utilize what you have learned.

Break out of your box! Act, think, in original ways. Find alternative ways of thinking and behaving. Wishing is better than apathy; constructive, organized thinking is better than wishing; positive action is best of all. Dag Hammar-skjöld said, "We act in faith, and miracles occur." If you reverse your mental and emotional attitudes and believe in yourself, you can handle anything.

Emotional Maintenance Inventory

The Emotional Maintenance Inventory will provide you with an ongoing evaluation of your emotional stability. With it, you will chart the highs and lows of your emotional cycles, before, during, and after your participation in the 3-Day Crash Program.

The Inventory is divided into five parts. They measure: Mood, Physical Symptoms, Attitudes Toward Self, Changes in Lifestyle, and Use of Drugs and Participation in Psychotherapies,

Sections I, II, and III score you from one to five for each item according to the way you have felt over the last three days. Simply choose the description which most accurately reflects your feelings and place its corresponding number on the blank line to the left of each item. Then add the scores on each line to obtain your total score for the section. On each of the first three sections you may obtain an Inventory score from 0 to 100.

Sections IV and V have point values assigned in parentheses for each item. For each life change that has occurred over *the last six months* place the point value for that item

23

on the line to the left of each item. Drug use is measured over the last month, and psychotherapy over the last year. After you have completed all five sections, add up your point total from each section to derive your current Emotional Maintenance Inventory Score.

The Emotional Maintenance Inventory is designed to assess your level of emotional stability before you begin the Crash Program and Lifelong Maintenance Program outlined in the next chapters. You are urged to compute your Inventory score right now so that it can be compared with your score upon completion of the 3-Day Crash Program and at various regular intervals when you will be testing yourself in the future.

The following table is a translation of your numerical score:

0–200 You have normal cycles of depression and anxiety but you appear to be coping well with them.

200–300 You are emotionally stable with normal mood swings, but you are feeling the pressures imposed by stress, or life changes, or unresolved emotional states. The EMM Lifelong Maintenance Program will help you clarify and resolve your problems.

300–500 You are suffering from emotional stress which needs attention before it develops into a major emotional illness. The 3-Day Crash Program is designed explicitly for you, to be followed by the Lifelong Maintenance Program.

500 & Above Your level of emotional instability is dangerously high at this point. You have a great many recent life changes and your coping mechanisms are becoming overworked. Try the Inventory again. If your score remains at or near its current level, you should consider professional help.

Emotional Maintenance Inventory

I. Mood

Please rate your feelings for the last three days along the following scales. Choose that description that best reflects your feelings in general for the last three days.

		Never	Just occasionally	Some of the time	Quite often	Most of the time	Always
___	1. I have felt sad	0	1	2	3	4	5
___	2. I have felt restless	0	1	2	3	4	5
___	3. I have felt angry	0	1	2	3	4	5
___	4. I have felt suspicious	0	1	2	3	4	5
___	5. I have felt frustrated	0	1	2	3	4	5
___	6. I have felt nervous	0	1	2	3	4	5
___	7. I have felt energetic	5	4	3	2	1	0
___	8. I have felt lonely	0	1	2	3	4	5
___	9. I have felt discouraged	0	1	2	3	4	5
___	10. I have felt tense	0	1	2	3	4	5
___	11. I have felt worried	0	1	2	3	4	5
___	12. I have felt guilty	0	1	2	3	4	5
___	13. I have felt embarrassed	0	1	2	3	4	5
___	14. I have felt like concentrating	5	4	3	2	1	0
___	15. I have felt calm	5	4	3	2	1	0
___	16. I have felt self-conscious	0	1	2	3	4	5
___	17. I have felt pessimistic	0	1	2	3	4	5
___	18. I have felt helpless	0	1	2	3	4	5
___	19. I have felt frightened	0	1	2	3	4	5
___	20. I have felt tired	0	1	2	3	4	5

_____ TOTAL   Score range: 0–100

II. Physical Manifestations:

		Never	Just occasionally	Some of the time	Quite often	Most of the time	Always
___	1. I have felt nauseous	0	1	2	3	4	5
___	2. I have had constipation or diarrhea	0	1	2	3	4	5
___	3. I have had difficulty breathing	0	1	2	3	4	5
___	4. I have felt a general tightness in my body	0	1	2	3	4	5
___	5. I have had a poor appetite	0	1	2	3	4	5
___	6. I have had difficulty sleeping	0	1	2	3	4	5
___	7. I have headaches	0	1	2	3	4	5
___	8. I have felt dizzy	0	1	2	3	4	5
___	9. I have had backaches	0	1	2	3	4	5
___	10. I have to urinate often	0	1	2	3	4	5
___	11. I have had discomfort in the abdomen	0	1	2	3	4	5
___	12. I have tremors in the hands or face	0	1	2	3	4	5
___	13. I have felt weak	0	1	2	3	4	5
___	14. My palms have felt sweaty	0	1	2	3	4	5
___	15. I have noticed my heart pounding	0	1	2	3	4	5
___	16. I have had blurred vision	0	1	2	3	4	5
___	17. I have had pains in the shoulders or neck	0	1	2	3	4	5
___	18. I have felt tired	0	1	2	3	4	5
___	19. I have had large mood swings	0	1	2	3	4	5
___	20. I have had little interest in sex	0	1	2	3	4	5
_____	TOTAL	Score range: 0–100					

III. Attitudes Toward Self

		Never	Just occasionally	Some of the time	Quite often	Most of the time	Always
___	1. I am well-liked by others	5	4	3	2	1	0
___	2. I am attractive to the opposite sex	5	4	3	2	1	0
___	3. I am a responsible person	5	4	3	2	1	0
___	4. I am able to express my emotions freely	5	4	3	2	1	0
___	5. I am an impulsive person	0	1	2	3	4	5
___	6. I put on a false front	0	1	2	3	4	5
___	7. I am an assertive person	5	4	3	2	1	0
___	8. I am a rational person	5	4	3	2	1	0
___	9. I am a hard worker	5	4	3	2	1	0
___	10. I am an unreliable person	0	1	2	3	4	5
___	11. I am an insecure person	0	1	2	3	4	5
___	12. I have a good personality	5	4	3	2	1	0
___	13. I am a relaxed person	5	4	3	2	1	0
___	14. I am a failure in many ways	0	1	2	3	4	5
___	15. I have trouble controlling aggressions	0	1	2	3	4	5
___	16. I am a confused person	0	1	2	3	4	5
___	17. I am contented	5	4	3	2	1	0
___	18. I am an ambitious person	5	4	3	2	1	0
___	19. I am an intelligent person	5	4	3	2	1	0
___	20. I just don't respect myself	0	1	2	3	4	5
_____	TOTAL	Score range 0–100					

In the blank space to the left of each life change put the point value in parentheses if that change has occurred in your life over the last six months.

IV. Changes in Life Style

(50) _____ 1. Divorce or separation
(50) _____ 2. Death in immediate family
(40) _____ 3. Job change
(35) _____ 4. Moved
(35) _____ 5. Personal injury or illness
(35) _____ 6. Marriage
(30) _____ 7. Retirement
(25) _____ 8. Pregnancy
(20) _____ 9. Sex difficulties
(20) _____ 10. Change in financial state
(20) _____ 11. Death of close friend
(15) _____ 12. Change in responsibilities at work
(15) _____ 13. Mortgage or loan over $15,000
(15) _____ 14. Outstanding personal achievement
(15) _____ 15. Begin or end school
(10) _____ 16. Revision of personal habits (dress, manners, associations, etc.)
(10) _____ 17. Change in social activities
(10) _____ 18. Change in form of recreation
(10) _____ 19. Change in sleeping habits (more or less, or change in hour)
(10) _____ 20. Change in eating habits (more or less intake, or change in hour)

_____   TOTAL   Score range 0–470

In the blank space on the left, enter the point value in parentheses if you have used the drugs listed below over the last month or participated in psychotherapy over the last year.

V. Drugs and Psychotherapy

Have you started using any of the following drugs in the last year: or if you already use them, have you progressively increased your usage:

(10) _____ 1. Alcohol

(10) _____ 2. Amphetamines (Benzedrine, Dexedrine, any form of "speed" or diet pill)

(10) _____ 3. Barbiturates (Amytal, Nembutal, Tuinal, Seconal)

(10) _____ 4. Tranquilizers (Librium, Valium, Thorazine)

(10) _____ 5. Narcotics (Opium, Heroin, Morphine)

(10) _____ 6. Antidepressants (Ritalin, Tricyclic Antidepressants)

(10) _____ 7. Marijuana

(10) _____ 8. Psychedelics (LSD, STP, PCP, Psilocybin)

(10) _____ 9. Aspirin

(10) _____ 10. Nicotine or caffeine

(10) _____ 11. Any other

Have you undergone any of the following forms of therapy in the past year:

(10) _____ 1. Psychoanalysis

(10) _____ 2. TA (Transactional analysis)

(10) _____ 3. Gestalt

(10) _____ 4. est (Mind dynamics, Scientology)

(10) _____ 5. Existential or Humanistic Therapy

(10) _____ 6. Behavior Therapy

(10) _____ 7. Jungian Analysis

(10) _____ 8. Rational Emotive Therapy

(10) _____ 9. Hypnotherapy

(10) _____ 10. Marriage or Family Therapy

(10) _____ 11. Primal Therapy

(10) _____ 12. Any Other

_____ TOTAL

PART II

The EMM
3-Day
Crash Program

Revving Up
and Breaking In

The Emotional Maintenance Manual's 3-Day Crash Program is a detailed, intensive course designed to increase your level of emotional self-awareness and overcome the tensions and anxiety that often result in depression, and to prepare you to deal with stress that arises from life crises and changes. The program *will* work for you but only if you are willing to alter your present living patterns in any way necessary. Following the program to the letter is no small task, and commitment is imperative if you are to make the adjustments required to increase your emotional stability and self-control.

These three days may be the most important of your life. All of your time and energy during this period will have to be devoted to the goal at hand—the creation of a more alive and aware *you*. In order to do this, a certain amount of preparation is required before beginning the program.

Read this section and the 3-day program itself at least four days before you plan to begin. This will allow time for you to acquire the necessary materials and prepare them for use in the program.

The Program entails three full days and it is recommended that you begin on a Friday morning and continue through Saturday and Sunday. Or you may want to start on a Saturday and continue through Sunday and Monday. In either case, it will be necessary for most people to excuse themselves from their jobs for at least one day. You may work the Program alone, with a friend, or in a small group.

Since the Program involves some exercise and dietary changes, you should have a medical checkup and your doctor's permission before embarking on it.

The day prior to beginning the Program, you should fast. The day before that, eat foods from the following categories only:

Lean meat, chicken or fish.
Eggs (not more than twice a week).
Vegetables, particularly dark green and deep yellow ones.
Fruits and a large measure of carbohydrates * is essential.
(Sixty percent of your diet should be in fruits and vegetables.)

* Recent research on the effects of dietary carbohydrates on brain chemistry may account for a recent report on a group of people suffering from narcolepsy—a condition marked by frequent and uncontrollable need for short periods of sleep. It was found that their condition became progressively worse with a diet of sweets (high sugar content). The mechanism, which has been worked out by an M.I.T. research team is as follows: It has been found in animals that ingestion of pure carbohydrate leads acutely to an increase in brain uptake of tryptophan from the blood. Tryptophan is one of the essential amino acids. When more tryptophan is taken into the brain, serotonin synthesis is stimulated, and brain levels of serotonin rise. Serotonin is a putative brainstem neurotransmitter which has been implicated in the maintenance of NREM sleep and in the primary stage of REM sleep. Depletion of serotonin from the brains of cats results in insomnia, a condition which can be reversed by replenishing serotonin supplies with the administration of the immediate precursor of serotonin, 5-hydroxytryptophan. Serotonin synthesis depends on the supply of L-trytophan to the brain. Oral administration of L-tryptophan has been repeatedly demonstrated to cause increases in subjective sensations of sleepiness in humans and to shorten the time needed to fall asleep after lights-out during polygraphic EEG recording. The M.I.T. researchers found that the higher brain serotonin levels in animals depended on a complex set

Whole-grain bread.

Brown rice or potatoes with skins.

Fluids without sugar (water, milk, juices).

The foods listed below under No. 9.

(This is a partial list, based on a more complete one given on pages 138–40. You will be eating only foods from this list through the three days of the crash program.)

You will need to obtain the following materials before embarking on the 3-Day Crash Program:

1. A half-dozen 4″ × 6″ index cards.
2. A felt-tipped marking pen.
3. Four notebooks—any style is acceptable (optional).
4. Tape recorder.
5. Comfortable clothes for exercise, including athletic shoes.
6. Colored pens.
7. Whistle.
8. Oxygen tank (LIFE-O-GEN, available in small tanks from pharmacies without prescription; or, preferably, rent a tank of compressed oxygen for $20 to $25 a month from your local medical equipment supplier).
9. Brewer's yeast, wheat germ, plain yogurt, nuts, fruits including bananas, bran cereal, and a supply of multivitamin, multimineral tablets including B complex, L-tryptophan, E, C, Sodium Potassium, Calcium, and Magnesium.

Some of the activities in the 3-Day Crash Program will be familiar to you and are therefore quite simple to under-

of effects of insulin, whose secretion is triggered by a pure carbohydrate meal. Conversely, it might be noted that a meal of high protein does not increase brain serotonin levels as it puts too many other amino acids into the bloodstream which can compete more effectively than tryptophan for uptake into the brain. Overall, one might predict that a pure glucose meal would lead to a rise in brain tryptophan and serotonin and thus an increase in calmness.

stand. Others will require some advance explanation before you undertake them. The following section outlines the activities and will explain those activities which might be new to you.

1. *Affirmation Cards*

These contain words that, although short and commonplace, are loaded words, words charged with meaning. They are abstract, that is, not defining anything concrete. Six such words were chosen, because when you think about them and everything they mean to you, they force you to come in contact with and recognize your feelings. They are: FEEL, EXPLORE, FIND, CARE, TRUST, LOVE. Print one in large letters on each of your index cards. You will be working with them throughout the program.

2. *Exercise Routines*

An integral part of the 3-Day Crash Program is the implementation of physical activity for overcoming the emotional lows of depression and anxiety. The importance of an exercise routine cannot be overemphasized if you are to successfully complete the program.

We have spent a good deal of time so far discussing various physiological and biochemical components of emotional behavior. Mind and body work in tandem and a healthy body is a prerequisite for emotional stability.

By now nearly everyone who is at all concerned about his or her body has experienced or at least heard about the extraordinary effect that physical exercise can have on the emotions. We hear about the "high" that joggers feel; about the euphoria that follows physical activity. Now we know the reason for this: physical activity activates adrenaline which in turn activates production of the neurotransmitters norepinephrine and serotonin, which *fight depression*. There is nothing better than exercise, therefore, when you are depressed or just emotionally sluggish.* A cost-free, completely healthy form of medication, exercise has only one side effect: because it causes arteries to the heart to grow in size, and because it creates new routes for carrying blood to the heart where coronary arteries are blocked, it can prevent heart disease! (Leonard, Hofer, Pritilcin, 1974).

In the 3-Day Crash Program, you will be given a choice of several physical activities to perform at various times throughout the day. Choose that activity which is best suited to your own constitution and current level of conditioning. You may want to experiment with several of the activities, but keep in mind that the exercise you perform is one of the most important components of the program for gaining and maintaining emotional stability.

---

* *Time* Magazine recently reported that several studies indicate that exercise works well for moderately depressed patients. In one test of 28 depressed patients, a team of psychiatrists and psychologists at the University of Wisconsin Medical School found that for most of them, 30 to 45 minutes of jogging three times a week was at least as effective as talk therapy. Psychiatrist Robert S. Brown of the University of Virginia at Charlottesville, who says it dawned on him one day that "nobody jogging down at the track ever appeared depressed" finds that exercise works better than pills in controlling depression. About 70 percent of all his patients, he says, are depressives, and all but 15 percent to 20 percent show "quick benefit" after only a week of running. Says U.C.L.A. Psychiatrist Ronald M. Lawrence: "mild depression is more common than the common cold, but it can be markedly helped by slow endurance exercise."

Some doctors believe that running cures mental problems by changing the chemical composition of the body. A. H. Ismail, professor of physical education at Purdue University, reports "significant relationships" between changes in certain hormone levels of joggers and improvements in emotional stability. Some critics think the joggers he studied, a group of out-of-shape professors, could have felt better simply because they were getting away from their desks for a change, but Ismail doubts that theory. Psychiatrist Brown thinks running fights depression by inducing chemical changes in the brain and he is now working with researchers at the National Institute of Mental Health.

3. *Oxygen Therapy*

The brain will die in minutes if it is deprived of oxygen, that's how essential it is to your very existence. The air we breathe is dirty, full of pollutants. It is recommended that you breathe pure oxygen for three minutes every morning and evening.

4. *Nutrition*

Proper diet and the intake of key nutrients is obviously important for maintaining physical and emotional well-being. The diet prescribed for the 3-Day Crash Program is designed to supply the body with the proper amounts of those nutrients which have been scientifically demonstrated to increase energy level and neurotransmitter effectiveness, and thereby affect emotional behavior. Tryptophan, an amino acid which is a precursor of serotonin, is found in most protein and B-complex vitamins. B-complex vitamins generally are responsible for the health and maintenance of your nervous system; they are found naturally in most concentrated form in brewer's yeast and wheat germ. Yogurt contains more B vitamins than milk. Bran aids digestion, providing roughage. Bananas contain a large amount of potassium, which combines with tryptophan to make serotonin.

During the 3-Day Crash Program we suggest no wine or cheese, since some types actually slow down or restrict the activity of the neurotransmitters. Although research on the subject is not conclusive enough for us to recommend that you eliminate them completely from your diet, it is suggested that should you fall into a low period sometime in the future, you would do well to cut them out.

Unless medication is prescribed by a doctor, we recommend no aspirin, tranquilizers, or antibiotics. We recommend four multivitamin, multimineral tablets per day.

5. *Relaxation Routines*

Since ancient times, man has been aware of the fact that he is able to control his physiological functions through mental activity such as meditation. Those who are well versed in the Eastern techniques of concentration are often able to achieve mental states which result in a lower pulse rate and slower respiratory and metabolic functioning. In short, they are able to slow down their bodily activities. By attaining a state of total relaxation, you will allow the body a chance to prepare itself for the stress and strain of most daily activities. The 3-Day Crash Program outlines a relaxation technique whereby anyone can achieve that state.

6. *Whistle*

You are to use your whistle throughout the 3-Day Crash Program to condition yourself to avoid negative thinking. For instance, you have an ache in your arm, and you begin to wonder about it: "what if" it is cancer . . . a heart attack . . . it will have to be amputated. Or you think your girlfriend was rather cold to you on the phone: "what if" . . . someone else was there . . . she doesn't care . . . I'll be all alone. This sort of thinking is termed obsessive, and although it is not serious in the examples given here, it is nonetheless defeatist, and it saps your emotional energy. Keep the whistle close at hand for the next three days. Hang it on a string around your neck—be your own lifeguard. Whenever you feel yourself falling into a negative thought track, blow your whistle loud and clear. It might sound silly, but what you are doing is conditioning yourself, just as Pavlov's dogs were conditioned. With that whistle toot, you are shocking yourself when a useless, negative thought pattern starts to develop.

The whistle is a signal of your ability to control your own life. Don't be embarrassed to blow it—whenever. It serves to remind you of your resolution to overcome negative thoughts, to replace them with positive thoughts. Sounding your whistle is a cue for these positive thoughts to enter consciousness. And thought precedes action!

7. Mood Clinic

The Mood Clinic is a unique and comprehensive set of mental exercises which allows you to observe your own attitudes and activities throughout the day. In effect, it is an organized method of introspection, in which you will learn to visualize, evaluate, and meditate upon your recent thoughts and reactions and rehearse alternative strategies for dealing with the same or similar situations. You can create roads where there weren't any before. We want you to think of the Mood Clinic as a mental gymnasium in which you can practice various combinations of emotional responses before expressing them publicly.

Since your Mood Clinic is a piece of equipment like the others you will be using during the 3-Day Crash Program, you should prepare it in advance. To bring it into being, close your eyes. Now create in your mind a setting: a house on a clean windswept beach, or a modern apartment high above a city, or a country cabin deep in a green forest or perched on a snowy mountain—any place that is pleasant to you and very secure and private. Within this location, create a room. Soundproof, comfortable, large, aesthetically pleasing. Pay attention to detail, see it coming into being, and design this room exactly as you want it to be.

You will have created a workshop where you can meditate, study, and plan possible courses of action for any situation. At various points during the 3-Day Crash Program, you will be asked to bring this mental room into existence and to visualize different activities within it.

(We must here stress the importance of procuring a tape recorder, if you do not already own one, for some of the Mood

Clinic activities. Do this before beginning the program so that you may concentrate all your energies on each day's programmed activities.)

Now you will need to concentrate intensively and imagine your room equipped with the following materials:

A. Chair and Table—the chair should be comfortable and to your liking since you often sit in this chair. You should also build a panel into the arm of the chair to control lighting and temperature. The table should be circular and designed for conference use.

B. Telephone—large, executive type, with several buttons to get direct lines anywhere in the world, plus several extensions and a TV screen so that you can see who you're talking to.

C. Clock and Calendar—capable of going backward or forward in time at the touch of a button to either review the past and see what made a certain situation a failure or success or to go into the future to plan 100 percent.

D. Files and Reference Books—on subjects such as analyses of situations and sets of circumstances; family history; biographies of those close to you; your own autobiography and health records, your finances, etc. The information should be encyclopedic, and as exact and precise as possible.

E. Platform and Screen—these are to be placed at the far end of your workshop, opposite your chair. Make the platform large enough to support a person, for you can summon anyone you want onto it. The screen is directly behind the platform. On the screen, you can create or re-create any setting, any situation you want. Switches for overhead lighting to illuminate the platform, and controls to activate the screen, should be located on the arm of your chair.

F. Elevator—to be placed to the right of your platform.

Use it to bring in anyone or anything that you may need from the past, present, or future. Place the door control of this elevator on the arm of your chair.

On Day 1 of the 3-Day Crash Program you will do various exercises to stretch your imagination, to teach you how to use the Mood Clinic. On Days 2 and 3 you will be instructed on how best to use the Mood Clinic to solve conflicts in relationships and resolve crisis situations.

It is a unique therapeutic tool designed to help you problem-solve, reflect, clear up, understand situations. Any problems, any person can be brought into the Clinic, where you will then be able to discuss, talk over, and communicate effectively and clearly—with yourself and with others.

8. *Reading Assignments, Charts, Tests, Exercises*

Each day you will be assigned various tests and exercises that will measure different aspects of your emotional self, and thereby help you see yourself from different points of view. On Day 1 you will read a short section outlining the history of and recent developments in understanding mind-body harmony, to acquaint you with the determinants of emotion.

9. *Play*

Most of us virtually stop playing at some point in our lives, but we never outgrow our need for it. Play not only keeps us young, it maintains our sense of perspective about the relative seriousness of things. Play is momentary escape from everyday cares and it also decreases their importance. Look after your sixth sense: your sense of humor. Play can be games, it can be structured relaxation, or it can be doing nothing, what is called "quiet time" in kindergarten. The form your play takes can be varied: a walk through the park, a visit to a museum, a volleyball game with the teenagers in the school-yard, doing a puzzle. Get in touch with the child within you before it disappears for good. You can't work all the time; all work and no play makes Jack a dull man. Play is instinctive in us. Get out of those "meetings," out of those cubicles, stop protecting your territory, your power, your image. Laughter ventilates your emotions.

10. *Travel Log*

The Travel Log is a technique through which you can discover within yourself the resources you did not know you possessed. As it is used over a period of time, it enables you to see a pattern in your life. Events and relationships unfold in its pages and reveal themselves for what they really were, what their real purpose was in your life, and what they wish to tell you for your future. As you leaf back through the pages of your Travel Log, you will gradually discover that your life *has* been going somewhere, however blind you have been to that direction and however unhelpful you yourself have been in that journey.

This diary can be used actively and intensively during times of conflict and difficulty or it may be used occasionally and with shorter entries when life is more relaxed. At certain points in the cycle of your experience, you may let it fall into temporary disuse.

The Travel Log is divided into four sections. You may either use one notebook for each section and write your thoughts down, or you may wish to dispense with the notebooks altogether and use the tape recorder. Do whatever seems easier and more comfortable for you.

The first section, called the Journey Plan, will be used to record the present phase of your life. It may cover a short period, such as the last few days, or a longer time, such as the last few months or so. You should use the Journey Plan to record the experiences that have led up to the present moment and how they may have come about. Ask yourself the question, "Where am I now in my life?" The answer to this question will provide the boundaries for your Journey Plan, how far it extends into the past and what events mark it off. Perhaps this recent period began when you had an idea for a new project. Or perhaps it began when you married, or had a child, or had a rift in your marriage relationship. Perhaps it has been a time of hard work, a time of confusion, or a time of waiting.

Record entries in your Journey Plan in brief form. Try to limit yourself to factual observations. The details of these experiences will be recorded in the next section of the diary.

This second section, your second notebook, is called Snapshots, and is an amplification and clarification of those events recorded in the Journey Plan. In Snapshots, you will record whatever images, impressions, or feelings you associate in your mind with the events you recorded in the first section. This sort of imagining must be done in a nonguided, nonconscious way, with the flow of feelings neither manipulated nor directed.

The third section of the Travel Log most clearly resembles the traditional view of a diary. This section, called the Daily Log, is essentially a running record of all the subjective experiences of all kinds that move through your mind and emotions in the course of a day and a night. It is similar to a diary in the respect that you will record entries in it regularly and on a continuing basis.

This is most easily accomplished by allowing some time at the end of each day to recall and recreate the events of the day. Then think back and record your feelings and thoughts about those events, both consciously and in your dreams. Take note of all the small details as they return to memory and record each briefly in the Daily Log.

The fourth and final section of the Travel Log is called Intersections: Roads Taken and Not Taken. By analyzing your own part in events recorded in the Journey Plan and

Snapshots, and by keeping track of your current experiences through the Daily Log, it will become apparent that your life is marked by a number of situations in which you were compelled to make important decisions. These are the intersection points of your life. Very often, at those moments of choice, the signposts were unclear. The information available to you was very limited, and you had no way of knowing what sort of terrain lay further along the road you chose. Yet, certain choices had to be made and must still be made because of that past decision. The Intersections part of the Travel Log allows you to record the circumstances surrounding these decision-making moments of your life; the alternatives you could have chosen, and how your actual decision has affected your life.

These brief descriptions of the four sections of the Travel Log will be further elaborated as each section is put into use in the 3-Day Crash Program. For the moment, all you will need are four properly labeled notebooks.

11. *Contract*

Upon your graduation from the Program, you will draw up a contract with yourself. In it, you will commit yourself to a long-range goal, reached through a series of smaller goals that are promises to yourself.

Each of the elements built into the 3-Day Crash Program treats a separate aspect of your emotional make-up: all together they add up to a coherent, dynamic plan that will, if you give it your best shot, lift you out of your complacent, defeatist, unclear, unproductive, finally self-defeating way of dealing with yourself and the world around you.

Wash out your system with plenty of water and fruit juices. When you're ready, turn off the telephone, plan three uninterrupted days to be alone and begin the program.

If it is at all possible, try to take the program away from the city. In the mountains, near the ocean, wherever there is green land and fresh clean air where you can be a part of nature. Dr. Albert P. Krueger, Professor and Chairman in the Department of Bacteriology at University of California at Berkeley has done amazing research on the quality of air and emotional health. According to Dr. Krueger, "We live in an ocean of air; in order to live we must breathe in and out at least 10,000 liters of air every day. Despite our dependence on air, we tend to ignore it until the toxic particles and gases that invade our atmospheric sea assault our eyes or lungs. The threat to life posed by heavy black industrial fumes is obvious, but there are subtle changes in the composition of the atmosphere that may also be detrimental to life and health. Among these invisible elements of the air is the phenomenon known as air ions."

Air ions are atmospheric gases that take on positive or negative charges. They are formed when energy produced by radioactive elements in the soil or by cosmic rays causes a gaseous molecule to lose an electron. The freed electron attaches to an adjacent molecule and the original molecule then has a positive charge, its neighbor, a negative one. Water vapor, oxygen, and hydrogen molecules cluster about the charged particle to form a "small air ion." The speed with which air ions form and recombine to neutralize their charges means there can be, at most, several thousand ions per cubic centimeter of air. The same cubic centimeter contains about 10 million trillion uncharged particles.

Hippocrates was correct in his observation that many people are sensitive to changes in the weather, but the role of air ions in their discomfort was not suspected until some 2,000 years later. In the last half of the 18th century, T. F. d'Alibard in France and Benjamin Franklin in the United States independently showed that there was electricity in the atmosphere, and several naturalists linked electricity with biological effects.

An article in *New West* Magazine suggests that the implications of Krueger's work are staggering. Positive ions are known to be bad for you causing insomnia, irritability and tension, while negative atmospheric ions can stimulate and increase energy levels and improve mental alertness. Over the decades, Krueger has been joined by distinguished scientists from Israel, Argentina, Japan, France, and the U.S.S.R. They have been remarkably thorough in detailing the genesis, history, and development of the ion and ion research.

The article asserts the earth itself carries a slight negative electrical charge, and is responsible for some atmospheric ionization. Both conditions are primarily the result of energy emission from radioactive substances in soil and rock.

Because like charges repel each other and opposite charges attract, an electrical drift in the air develops. Weak banks of polarity form, with the positive ions hovering closer to the ground and the negative ones rising to higher altitudes. For example, up to 48 hours before clouds appear, the early winds arrive, stirring up dust and particulates, bringing sore muscles, migraines, uneasy sleep, and short tempers to one-third to one-half of the population. Rain follows, cleaning the air of particulates. The larger raindrops absorb positive charges and carry them into drains. Smaller drops retain negative charges and float more readily on the air. As the storm passes, the rain turns to a drizzle, and the negative atmospheric ion content shoots up. Spirits rise. Indoors, kids and kittens get skittish. Employees near open windows whistle while they work.

Moving into the body, atmospheric ions induce functional changes in the adrenal, pituitary, and thyroid glands. In addition, negative and positive ions respectively lower and raise the body level of serotonin, the powerful neurohormone connected with sleep, nerve impulse transmission, and mood. Taken as an interactive whole, these changes are at once so subtle and powerful that few of their final effects have been spelled out so accurately as to enjoy a complete scientific imprimatur.

- Ions are biologically active, affecting living matter from bacteria to human beings.

- Depletion of ions in the air may increase a person's susceptibility to illnesses like respiratory infections.
- An increase in ions and particularly in the ratio of negative to positive ions may be useful in the treatment of burns and respiratory diseases.
- Conditions in urban centers, characterized by air pollution outdoors and artificially controlled climate indoors, lower the total number of small ions in the air and decrease the negative-to-positive ion ratio.

Theories about the effects of air ions fit neatly with observations of natural phenomena. Work in France, Germany, Italy, and the Soviet Union on the ionic environment of spas, particularly those located near waterfalls, has shown that the air in many spas near mountain ranges and open space has a high concentration of air ions and an unusually high ratio of negative to positive ions. Air at the seashore also has a high level of air ions. Of course, people visit spas, beaches, and waterfalls for many reasons, but the beneficial effects of air ions may prove to be one of them. Dr. Krueger and his researchers feel that negative ions affect our moods and accelerate the delivery of oxygen to our cells and tissues.

Before you embark on the 3-Day Crash Program, I would like to emphasize that some of the techniques and exercises may seem initially directionless. However, the Program has been carefully designed. These emotional exercises are much like physical exercise; they create an emotional tone—mental circulation—to shape, firm, and condition you mentally and emotionally.

We affect our exterior world by our interior environment. The 3-Day Crash Program is designed to shape the framework of your emotional architecture. The results of the program are accumulative. Some exercises will yield immediate benefits; others will prove useful during the Lifelong Maintenance Program. All are structured to increase your self-awareness, your understanding of others, and provide emotional balance in your life.

Lastly, be sure you appraise your physician that you are taking the program. You want to be sure that there are no medical, dietary, and exercise restrictions which would apply to you.

Day 1

7:00 A.M.:　Time to wake up and begin the day's activities. Immediately upon awakening breathe pure oxygen for 5 minutes from your oxygen supply. This is optional but strongly recommended especially if your live in a smog-filled climate. Then place Affirmation Card 1, with the word FEEL printed on it, in a prominent place in your bedroom. Sit on a chair, bed, or the floor, where you can see the card clearly. Concentrate on the word printed on the card. What does the word mean to you? What are feelings? Are they nerve impulses sent from your brain, and acted upon by your judgment? Are they the result of external stimuli? Internal? What is it like not to feel? How do you feel most of the time? Have you ever had a feeling so special it happened only once or twice in your life? What was it like? Think about how you feel toward inanimate things, like your house or apartment, your possessions, your garden, your pets. How have you made others feel, and how, in turn, did that make you feel? In other words, think about yourself in relation to the word.

As you concentrate on this word you will unlock other

thoughts, feelings, and emotions. You will begin to understand how they are interrelated. Thoughts create feelings. Feelings create thoughts.

Feel. Realize there are choices and options. You really can choose to feel good or bad. Of course there are exceptions; traumatic events in life which we have little control over. We are always feeling and feeling is a part of living.

Understand why you feel. Discover insights: I feel because I love or I am hurt or I am frustrated.

Write down why you feel and how you feel, and from time to time refer to that report in quiet moments. In this way, you will revitalize your awareness of feelings and begin to incorporate this knowledge in your daily life. Spend five minutes thinking about FEEL and keep the word in mind for the next few hours.

7:05 A.M.: Put on your favorite record or tape, or listen to the wind in the trees outside, or the rain, or even the hushed roar of traffic—any constant, nonjarring sound—and relax for the next ten minutes. Concentrate on the sound as you continue to think about the word FEEL. Make yourself aware of your senses of sight, hearing, and touch as you listen to your sound.

7:15 A.M.: The next part of the morning will be spent in various forms of exercise. Remember what we discussed earlier: steady and sustained physical activity, the kind that ups your pulse rate, is, with diet, the best medicine you can take for depression or anything resembling it. Even if you just feel sluggish, without much mental and emotional energy, a few minutes of exercise will get you going—it's much healthier than a cup of coffee.

First, though, you will do some loosening-up exercises. While standing straight, bend over and touch your toes or reach as close to the floor as you possibly can. Stand up straight again. Repeat the toe touching exercise 20 times.

Now, while standing straight, place your hands on your

hips and twist your upper body in a circular motion so that your chest is making a complete circular motion, without moving your feet or legs. Feel the muscles stretch as you continue to twist your upper body forward, to the left, back, and to the right. Continue for three minutes.

7:30 A.M.:   Take the next ten minutes to get dressed for outdoor exercise (or in a bathing suit). You may dress in jogging clothes and running shoes or simply comfortable clothes with soft-soled shoes. Put your whisle in your pocket.

7:40 A.M.:   Now that your body feels loose and relaxed, it is time to engage in more strenuous exercise, depending on your degree of physical fitness.

If you don't know a thing about exercising, you should read the chapter "A Word about Cycles" before embarking today. For the future, outline a program for yourself based on one of the exercise paperbacks. There are four or five good ones on the shelves now.

The next 30 minutes are to be spent bicycling, or swimming laps if you have the use of a pool, or jogging or walking, or a combination of the latter two, called "roving." All of these exercises are "aerobic"—that is, they increase the pulse rate, stepping up both blood flow and adrenaline flow and releasing the antidepressant neurotransmitters. And more life-giving oxygen is sent to the brain. Don't sell this part of the program short! It's vitally important.

If, like most of us, you aren't in particularly good condition, you will probably choose roving for your exercise. You can do it anywhere—in a field, on the beach, on the city streets. Begin by jogging until you feel tired, then walk, and then jog some more. Look around you, enjoy yourself, think positively about your word FEEL. Remember to blow your whistle if a negative feeling creeps in.

8:10 A.M.:   Take a relaxing shower—not too hot or too cold —and get dressed for the day's activities. Don't forget your affirmation word during this period.

8:30 A.M.: Prepare yourself a breakfast which includes the following: fruit or fruit juice, one banana, bran cereal, honey and milk, a tablespoon of brewer's yeast. Start taking the vitamins described on page 38.

9:00 A.M.: Emotional Energy Output Chart

Emotional crises utilize an inordinate amount of your time and energy in nonproductive ways. The depressed or anxious individual may idle away the hours dwelling on past opportunities or the lack thereof. Excessive time and energy may also be spent on preparing for or wishfully thinking about the future. Fixating on the past or the future decreases the amount of available energy at your disposal for use in the present.

The Emotional Energy Output Chart provides a means for measuring your daily expenditure of energy and your allocation of time. A clearer understanding of the way you now use your time and energy can provide the impetus for its redistribution in a way that will be more profitable to you. Effective use of time and energy is vital for coping with life's daily dilemmas.

To use the chart, simply color in the number of hours spent on each activity. Hours are numbered from 0–24 on the left side of the chart. Color in one space for each hour you spend in a typical 24-hour period on each of the activities listed along the bottom of the chart. By using a different colored pencil for each of the twelve activities you can obtain a clear indication of how your time and energy is being distributed.

Your use of time can be a complicated issue. It is important to establish priorities in relationship to responsibility. You must establish a balance between needs, desires, and obligations.

A physician may spend too much time with his practice; a wife an inordinate amount of time in community activities; an artist in his work; the businessman with checks and bal-

	Career Social Relationships outside of family	Family	Education & other forms of self-improvement	Recreation— sports and hobbies	Community activities	Activities of daily living (eating, home, maintenance, grooming)	Passive activities (TV, movies, radio, spectator sports)	Anxiety or worry about the future	Depression or guilt as a result of the past	Sleep	Other
24											
23											
22											
21											
20											
19											
18											
17											
16											
15											
14											
13											
12											
11											
10											
9											
8											
7											
6											
5											
4											
3											
2											
1											
0											

ances; the athlete in training; the child at play. Each is oc-
cupied with his or her own area of concern—sometimes fulfilling—sometimes obsessive to the detriment of family,
career, or home.

As you prepare your chart, look at your present use of
time. Is the Energy Output Chart balanced? Where can you
adapt and compromise? What can you change? Be aware of
the patterns that reinforce your behavior. Very often we have
a vested interest in maintaining certain kinds of behavior, and
change becomes very difficult.

Your energy output should be in perfect balance with
your goals and responsibilities. In terms of priority and choice,
you must decide what is important to you and the relationship.

For example, if you are a person who is spending too
much time in community activities and not enough quality
time with your family, you may have to re-evaluate your goals,
responsibilities, and desires. Greater self-awareness should lead
to a more productive use of time and energy. When you know
what you *really* want, you can make appropriate decisions. To
this end, the exercises in this program will help. You can develop these issues in your Mood Clinic; you can recondition
negative behavior with tools for creating change. You can
develop a positive mode of behavior. You can take control and
be amazed at how easily you will be able to refocus your life.

After you have completed the charting of your emotional
energy output, consider its implications. Are you in fact
spending time on activities that detract from your living life
to its fullest? Are you spending excessive time and energy in
particular areas as a means of avoiding energy output in other
more demanding but more productive areas? You will be surprised at the number of hours you exhaust every day on activities that actually do not appeal to you, that may even
cause you distress.

On the second chart, on the following page, fill in your
own Ideal Emotional Energy Output, distributing your time

	Career Social Relationships outside of family	Family	Education & other forms of self-improvement	Recreation— sports and hobbies	Community activities	Activities of daily living (eating, home, maintenance, grooming)	Passive activities (TV, movies, radio, spectator sports)	Anxiety or worry about the future	Depression or guilt as a result of the past	Sleep	Other
24											
23											
22											
21											
20											
19											
18											
17											
16											
15											
14											
13											
12											
11											
10											
9											
8											
7											
6											
5											
4											
3											
2											
1											
0											

and energy in a more productive way. Compare your actual and ideal output charts and work to reduce the discrepancies. Examine the reasons for your current output level and redistribute your energy in a way that will be more emotionally gratifying to you.

After you have completed *The Emotional Maintenance Manual*'s crash program, you will want to keep weekly or monthly tabs on how your emotional energy is being distributed. By comparing charts you will be able to detect progress toward a more constructive use of time and energy that will benefit both you and others.

9:30 A.M.:   Spend the next hour exploring your innermost thoughts via the Travel Log. Begin your diary in the notebook entitled Journey Plan. This, you will recall, is used to record the most recent period of your life. For some, a starting point will seem immediately obvious: a crisis situation; a career change; a recent upheaval in a personal relationship. If no immediate thoughts come to mind, think about yourself in relation to other areas in your life—your family, your friends, your work, school, etc. What recent events or experiences in these areas stand out? Are these events marked by typical behavior patterns on your part?

For example, do you continually develop interpersonal relationships that have no chance of success? Many people, consciously or unconsciously, set themselves up for rejection. Consider the reasons behind such a behavior pattern—insecurity, fear of intimacy, need for punishment. And when the relationship once again fails, these negative belief systems are merely reinforced, and no attempt is made to discover the reasons and the source of such a pattern.

Choose a quiet spot and think about these questions. Memories will surface, reflecting the quality of movement, the direction your life has taken. Whatever form these memories take, let yourself perceive them. Do not reject, censor, or affirm them; certainly you should not interpret them.

Simply observe and record what comes to you. As you become more adept at this exercise, you will become increasingly aware of the inner continuity and movement of your life, and the cyclical nature of your behavior patterns. Record both the events and the memories of this recent period. Feel free to record whatever information you desire, but keep in mind that these entries are to be brief, so limit yourself to one hour in this first section of the Travel Log.

10:30 A.M.:   During the next 1½ hours, choose a favorite activity that takes you away from your home. You may want to go to a museum, spend time with someone you like, go to a book store, a zoo, or simply on a nature walk. Take along two stamped envelopes and notepaper, and don't forget to use your whistle if you have to.

12:00 noon: Take a long, relaxing lunch break. Stop by a favorite lunch spot. Select foods from the list on pages 138–40. While there, pay someone a deserved compliment—a patron or an employee of the restaurant. Notice the person's reaction to your compliment. Analyze why you think this particular reaction occurred; it will help you form the habit of considering what effect your words and attitudes have on others.

During or right after lunch, take the time to write two short letters, one to yourself and the other to someone close to you. In the letters, clearly express your feelings at the present moment. The letter to someone close to you may be either full of love or anger. The letter to yourself should be very personal. Mail both letters to you. This is just an exercise. I want you to see if your feelings are the same when you receive the letters in a few days. How do you feel about what you wrote. Doesn't it feel better to clarify your thoughts and ventilate your feelings . . . about someone else and about yourself?

1:15 P.M.:   Take a look at yourself in the mirror. Then make a list of the things you like about yourself. For example:

a. I am a good friend
b. I am loyal
c. I do a specific thing well
d. I am a feeling person
e. I have a sense of humor
f. I am logical in my approach to problem solving.

After you have made this list, glance at it over the next few days and congratulate yourself on your good qualities.

1:30 P.M.:   Inner Perception Test

Draw three boxes: 1 large box, 1 medium box, and 1 small box. Close your eyes, imagine something in the big box and draw a picture of that object or image. Now imagine that you are that drawing. Become it completely and from that point of view, not your own, fill in the blanks below:

1. I feel (descriptive activity) _____

   _____

2. I am (descriptive adjective) _____

   _____

3. I wish _____

4. I most secretly _____

5. I need _____

6. I will _____

Repeat the same process for the two other boxes. In each case, imagine the object, draw it, become it, and fill in the next two sets of statements.

1. I feel _____

2. I am _____

3. I wish _____

4. I most secretly _____

5. I need _____

6. I will _____

1. I feel _____
2. I am _____
3. I wish _____
4. I most secretly _____
5. I need _____
6. I will _____

Key:

The large box represents how you present yourself to the world; the image of yourself you allow the world to see. Compare those answers from that point of view.

The middle box represents your adult moderator, your rational thought processes. It is how you think logically about the world.

The small box represents your inner core, your secret self and how that secret self feels about the world and its relationship to it.

Think about this exercise. You may have gained some insight into yourself and your relationships.

2:00 P.M.: The next hour is to be spent on the mental exercises we described earlier, the Mood Clinic. To bring the Mood Clinic into existence, sit in a comfortable place, close your eyes, and relax. Then bring your secret house, cabin, or apartment into being. Sit in your specially prepared workshop, in your chair with the control buttons on the arm.

Today you will use your Mood Clinic just for exercise— to stretch your imagination and ready it for the work it will be doing later, when you will be examining your life situations and your reactions to them.

First you will exercise your visual imagination. Flip the switch on your chair that activates the big screen across from you. Now form an image on it of the first of the following descriptions, and view it for 30 seconds. Then move onto the next image, until you have visualized all ten.

1. Glass of iced tea with a large Number 1 painted on the side.
2. An old man with a white beard and the animals going into the Ark two by two.
3. The month of May, a country scene with a clump of three tall trees.
4. Four rays of light shining through a window with four panes of glass.
5. A policeman representing the law, with a large Number 5 badge on his chest.
6. A wrestler with a square, rugged jaw and six teeth sticking out from it.
7. A heavily engraved expensive gold key in the shape of a seven.
8. A large price tag for eight million dollars.
9. Water surrounded by land in the shape of a nine with the tail of the nine connecting the water to the ocean.
10. Your own ten toes.

Now you will extend your imagination a little further, using your other senses. Experience the following on your screen, adding sensations other than purely visual:

1. The smell of rain.
2. The feeling of the first day of fall, of football season.
3. A summer night.
4. Swimming in a warm, crystal-clear sea, the sand like velvet under your feet.
5. The sound of wind in pine trees.
6. The sound of the pounding surf.
7. The warmth of the sun on your body.
8. Eating your favorite dish, cooked to perfection, and served in your favorite way—on paper plates at the beach, or on Sevres china at Maxim's.

Imagine all of these sensations in detail: spend some time on each of them.

The next exercise will prepare you for the more difficult activity of emotional imagining: creating or re-creating feelings. Using the same equipment as before, imagine:

1. How you felt on the last day of school.
2. How you felt kissing someone you liked very much for the first time.
3. Receiving an unexpected phone call bringing very good news.
4. How you felt after accomplishing something difficult, like surfing in on a wave, or skiing down a hill for the first time, or passing your driving test.

Once again, spend some time on each experience and use as much sensory data as you can, because that will facilitate emotional imagining.

Now you will create some situations which contain extended and/or more complicated emotions, both your own and those of other actors in your Mood Clinic. This is a preparation for later use of your imagination to run through actual situations in your life that have been troubling you and need solving.

In the following exercises, you will be "modeling" behavior—as a sculptor models a lump of clay—modeling your own reactions as well as those of others. To do this you will have to take the roles of your other actors as well as your own; you will have to have multiple perspectives on the situation. You will "run through" these situations so that you can "know" them—this is the cognitive process of desensitizing emotions, making them less fearsome and overwhelming. Anxiety is fear of the unknown. You will have to project an outcome for the situation, evaluate and review your performance and those of other actors. This will then become a tool to reducing anxiety in an actual situation.

Your exercises and your real-life Mood Clinic sessions will fall into two categories: Relationships, and Situations or Events. These break down further into a) Conflict and b) Nonconflict relationships or situations.

Take several minutes for each of these exercises, imagine them in detail, and use all of the tools and equipment at your disposal: bring people onto your stage through the elevator, put on tapes, refer to your files and reference books, talk to experts over the phone, go back and forward in time as the exercise demands. Remember, the Mood Clinic is your workshop: it is a safe place to experiment, to take risks.

Set up a relationship of conflict between you and another person. Discuss with him/her what the barriers are between you. Ask what you can do to improve the quality of the relationship; how does the person react? Make your own demands. How does the person react to those? How do you feel? Are you angry? Sad? Confused? Afraid? Why? Can you change it? Can you say anything that will make the other person more sympathetic? What would he *like* to hear? Can you accommodate him/her without compromising yourself? Can you sway him then? Get another opinion from someone else; perhaps a concurring opinion from an expert whom you phone. Call upon your alter ego, your conscience—the inner person who is a part of you. Think about how you feel now. Think about how the other person feels. Is the outcome successful for both of you? Can you make it so? If you want to, do whatever you have to to resolve this conflict satisfactorily for both of you. If there is no way to do this, can you make your victory easier for the other person to accept, in order to keep him/her on your side in the future? Do you want to do this?

Set up a situation in which you have to build your courage, either with friends or strangers.

It can be a relatively minor confrontation: You are waiting in a long line at the cash register in a big department store. The cashier is very slow, and to make matters worse, when a stock boy brings her a supply of wrapping materials she stops working entirely to flirt with him. You are near the end of the line and not very close to the girl. You wait, but she doesn't go back to work. You wait some more: no one else says a word. It is embarrassing to yell out angrily across a space of perhaps twenty feet. You *could* report her to the manager afterward, or you *could* talk about her in a loud voice to your fellow-sufferers in line. Screw up your courage instead, and say something to her. Not angrily, not with embarrassment, but authoritatively, factually and short. How do you feel doing it? Afterward? Did it work? Could you have done something better? *

You might choose a life-changing confrontation: You need $25,000 to start a small business. You have the experience needed in the field, you have a perfect location, you have planned all the details. If you don't do it, someone else will, fast, and you don't feel things will ever come together again so opportunely for you. The best way to get the loan is to approach the owner of the company you now work for; it is, of course, in the same field, and you are a highly respected employee there. Of course, he won't want to lose you. He could possibly steal your idea—although you trust him, you can never be sure; he is a brusque, very rich and very powerful self-made man. Everyone is slightly frightened of him. You finally gather together your courage and go to see him. Imagine his office, his secretary. He could be someone you actually know, if that makes the scenario easier for you.

What will happen? Try confronting him with your normal self, then try a more dynamic, aggressive version of yourself. Think of the sort of man he is: surely this is a difficult situation for him, too. Put yourself in his chair: what is he feeling? Then react to that. Once again, use all of your tools and examine the situation from all sides.

At the end of this session, write down what you have

* We are all different. If this is not a difficult situation for you, envision another one. This is only one example.

discovered about yourself in relation to the world around you. If there are negative observations, include your insights about how you can change them. Note five to ten points. Read the list aloud to yourself. Carry it around with you. Make it a reality. If you practice a confrontation mentally it will become easier to put into actual practice. It is no more or no less a rehearsal, preparing and conditioning yourself to face an issue fairly. And you *will* have to face the initial assertive encounter, especially if it is in an area which has always been a problem for you. But these practice sessions should make that initial encounter somewhat less frightening.

3:00 P.M.: It's time to change your affirmation card. Replace the card FEEL with the second card, EXPLORE. Spend a few minutes thinking about how this word applies to your own life; relate it to the activities you have performed thus far today. Find new ways to think about exploration: as analysis; discovery; examination; familiarity; sorting out; dissection; searching for insights. How can you explore? You can gather all available information; you can consult experts; you can ask basic questions; you can search for repeated patterns; you can make theories.

3:15–4:15 P.M.: During the next hour, you are encouraged to express positive emotions toward a close friend, an acquaintance, or even a stranger. This exercise may take several forms. You may want to visit a sick friend, or drop by a local hospital or convalescent home to cheer someone up, even if that someone is a complete stranger. You may want to buy a small gift for someone. Or you can use your imagination and perform a visible or an anonymous good deed for someone. The important point is to express love and affection.

4:15 P.M.: Time for afternoon exercise. You have a choice of bicycling, jogging, roving, swimming. Don't overdo it, however. You know your body's limits so take short rests whenever necessary.

5:00 P.M.: Spend the next half-hour on the Day 1 reading assignment at the end of this chapter, on Mind/Body Theories and History.

5:30 P.M.: For the next half-hour, you will engage in relaxation exercises. Find yourself a comfortable position on the floor or a rug. Make sure nothing will impede the relaxation process. Now read over the remainder of this section until you understand completely what is required of you, then put it aside and concentrate fully on the relaxation technique.

Begin by closing your eyes and taking some deep breaths. Breathe slowly and deeply, and with each exhalation allow your body to become more and more loose. Breathe in and out and repeat the word R-E-L-A-X to yourself with each breath.

Now begin counting very slowly from 21 backward toward 1. As you slowly count, concentrate on the feeling of relaxation permeating steadily deeper within your body, easing tight, tense muscles. By the time you reach the number 1 your body will be in a state of complete and deep relaxation.

Now imagine a serene brook flowing alongside a lush green meadow. Project yourself onto the meadow. Feel the coolness of the grass and hear the soft gurgling of the stream as you lie back. Allow your mind to concentrate fully on the wonderful feelings of calm and well-being moving through your body. Continue to concentrate for the next few minutes. Before you move to the next activity, take a relaxing ten-minute shower to ease you back into the routine.

6:00 P.M.: Prepare yourself dinner from your list of acceptable foods.

7:00 P.M.: You have a choice of activities for the evening. Go out to a movie, the theater, or a concert. Don't forget your word, EXPLORE, and take along your whistle!

10:15 P.M.: At home, seat yourself in a quiet place with the notebook you have entitled Daily Log. Sit quietly, breathe slowly, regularly, and close your eyes, concentrating on the events and feelings of the last tweny-four hours. Remember how well you slept and what dreams you may have had. Think of the feelings you had just before dozing off and jot them down in the Daily Log.

When you awakened in the morning, how did you feel physically? Did you awaken slowly, as though you were emerging from a dream? Or did you awaken quickly, full of energy and alertness? What were your emotions and desires, anxieties and hopes?

How did you begin the tasks of the day? What were the thoughts that came unbidden to your mind? Were you aware of subconscious feelings and fantasies? Did you find yourself worrying about things that you did not want to be thinking of? Did you find hopes or wishes entering your mind without your consciously summoning them?

What were your interactions with others during the course of the day? Were there experiences of love and affection or frustration and anger? Let yourself feel again the emotions that arose in you and that were brought forth in others. Record them briefly and describe as well as you can the direction of your emotional responses and those of the other persons involved with you during the day.

Recall the variation in your feelings as your needs of the morning continued or changed at lunchtime, at midday, and as different people entered the scene. Consider how they varied in the latter part of the afternoon, and in the evening. What was your mood and the tempo of your thoughts and feelings at night, and as you now prepare for bed?

These questions may serve as a point of reference for recalling the events and accompanying feelings of the last twenty-four hours. When you use the Daily Log, do not inadvertently censor or edit the material you are recording. Do not exclude things because you are ashamed of them. Don't be concerned about grammar, literary style, or the use of political language. It is important, rather, that you feel free to write in your everyday language, letting the flow of words reach paper without editing or censorship. There is no length requirement in this exercise; record whatever seems right and comfortable for you.

When you have finished, sit quietly again, breathe slowly, and absorb the feelings that you have been describing.

11:00 P.M.: The end of Day 1 of the 3-Day Crash Program. Breathe oxygen for five minutes. Have a glass of milk. Take a warm bath, and prepare for bed. Once more, think over the affirmation cards you used during the day. Get a good night's sleep. Tomorrow is loaded with exciting, new experiences.

The EMM Crash Program Day-1 Reading Assignment

Mind-Body Harmony

The struggle to define the relationship between mind and body dates back to the beginning of civilization and continues unabated today. Are mind and body distinct entities or are they inextricably linked? Modern research has determined that we are influenced by our genetic code, our biochemistry, and our environment. At different places, at different times, these factors influence both our mind and body and create our individuality.

As early as 2,000 years ago, Chinese Confucian philosophy centered on the belief that mental and physical functions were interrelated and not localized in any one part of the body.

In 400 B.C. the Greek philosopher Plato wrote that discord between body and mind causes mental aberration. Plato's emphasis on mind-body harmony led him to speculate that physical activity was important in curing mental ills:

> *Exercise restores the sufferers to a state of inner calm*
> *and repose and brings them back to their sober senses.*
> *Thus, the inner tumult is cured by outer activity;*
> *unwholesome mania is driven out by beneficient*
> *mania, and in the end both kinds of mania are gone.*

Sound advice in light of what we now know about the benefits of physical exercise in relieving mental stress.

In later essays, Plato explained irrational events and behavior as an inevitable part of human life, rather than the product of evil spirits and other noxious influences. He attempted to subject these irrational actions to the rational control of the mind. Again his ideas are reflected in the many forms of modern psychotherapy that are based on cognitive control of behavior.

Aristotle also embraced the concept of the mind-body unit. His views differed substantially from those of Plato, however. Aristotle contended that an excess of black bile in the body resulted in mental illness—distorted sensory perception and hallucinations. His idea of an organic syndrome mediating between mind and body—called melancholia—has considerably influenced Western thought down through the ages.

Not all of the early cultures believed in the unity of mind and body. Many Eastern societies embraced superstitious causations of disease. The belief that spirits could enter the body to cause illness presupposes a consideration of the body and soul as distinct entities.

In the 5th century B.C., however, Alcmaeon of Croton believed the brain to be the seat of both the senses and the intellect. And Hippocrates, the father of modern medicine, stated in the 4th century B.C., that:

> *Men ought to know that from nothing else but thence (from the brain) come joys, delights, laughter, and sports; and sorrows, griefs, despondence, and lamentations. And by this in an especial manner, we acquire vision and knowledge, and we see and hear.*

As the foundations of psychology became more rational, the ideas of Plato and other Greek philosophers were widely acknowledged. During the 3rd century B.C., the Epicureans and Stoics emphasized moderation of the passions in every human act as the key to mental and physical well-being. Among the therapeutic methods employed by Greek and Roman physicians, word therapy became the most prevalent. Awareness of the power of the word in Greek culture coincided with their belief that life is governed by rational and logical principles that can be discovered and followed. Plato's emphasis on the need for harmony between body, psyche, and soul is reflected in the dialogues of Socrates who viewed the achievement of moderation and self-control as necessary for good behavior. In terms of therapy, moderation and self-control were to be achieved through the persuasive words of a man of prestige or, possibly, through the patient's self-expression. Many client-centered therapies today are based on the supposition that self-expression in the presence of an accepting therapist is a necessary step in the resolution of emotional conflict. Rational control of emotional behavior remains an important underlying assumption.

Psychological theories of the Middle Ages continued to be influenced by Aristotelian writings, which stressed the body-mind unity and, thus, the biological foundation of psychology. The theologian and philosopher St. Augustine subscribed to the widely accepted division of the mind into the three faculties of reason, memory, and will. He, like the Greek philosophers, felt that passions could be moderated by reason.

With the emphasis upon mind-body unity, physicians in the Middle Ages attempted to localize mental functions in various parts of the brain. Depression or melancholia was attributed to damaged faculties of the mind.

Arabic cultures in the Middle Ages were also influenced by Greek concepts of body and mind. The scholar Constantinus Africanus, founder of the renowned medical school of Salerno, prescribed proper diet, kind and sensible words, music, baths, rests, physical exercise, and sexual gratification as a cure for melancholia. He emphasized that emotions were considered the link between mind and body. Emotional ills might originate in the body, thus affecting the mind, and vice versa. Current research in psychosomatic medicine, viewed as the most natural expression of the body-mind interaction, confirms many of these theories.

The delicate science of neurochemistry has amassed an impressive body of evidence to support the theory that chemical reactions within brain cells control behavior. Increasingly sophisticated and precise research techniques have enabled investigators to probe the most deeply hidden aspects of the brain and observe the tiny workings of nature's most magnificent machine. Reseachers are giving up attempts to define which structures regulate behavior. Instead, they have started exploring the biochemical nature of the brain and have unveiled an extraordinarily complex system through which the brain sends and receives signals from all over the body. Some of the most fascinating work has concentrated on the regulation of emotions through the brain's biochemistry.

In the past twenty years, an exhausting amount of research has been devoted to finding the chemical basis of mental illness. In some instances, the search has proven exceedingly fruitful.

The emotional disorder which has received the most attention from biochemists is unquestionably that of depression. A formal theory of depression, the "biogenic amine hypothesis," has come to be regarded as the basic tenet of biological psychology. The theory has received almost universal support from a wide variety of studies.

In simple terms, this theory is based on the presence of chemicals which transmit emotional expressions to and from the emotional center of the brain. An example: Suppose you are taking a leisurely stroll through the neighborhood on a Saturday afternoon. You are relaxed and contemplating the excellent dinner you have planned for the evening. Suddenly, without warning, a large snarling dog bolts across a neighbor's yard, bounds over the fence, and comes rushing toward you. Your immediate reaction is fear. Certainly you haven't had time to think. Your behavioral response is to try to defend yourself or to escape as quickly as possible.

Whatever response you may have made in this or a similar situation was the product of an intricate wiring system in which the eyes were able to transmit the image of an angry dog to the brain which, in turn, directed the legs to run or the arms to reach for a nearby object. More specifically, the area of the brain responsible for signaling fear sent an impulse to the appropriate area of the body for taking action. The impulse itself is much like an electrical charge and is conducted along nerve tracts. The impulse makes its way from neuron (nerve cell) to neuron along the nerve tract. Between each neuron there is a minute gap which must be breached before the impulse can continue its transmission. As you have read earlier, the body provides chemical substances, called neurotransmitters, which surround each neuron and fill the gaps between them thus allowing the nerve impulse to travel from—in our example—the eyes to the hypothalamus to the legs.

Specific kinds of neurotransmitters, norepinephrine, dopamine, and serotonin, have most often been implicated in affecting emotional moods. This information is based on studies which demonstrated below-normal concentrations of neurotransmitters in the spinal fluid and other body fluids of depressed patients. Various forms of therapy, including electroshock, tend to increase levels of neurotransmitters so the patient improves.

Studies of antidepressant drugs provide further evidence. Essentially these drugs fall into two categories—the monoamine oxidase inhibitors and the tricyclic antidepressants. Administration of both categories of drugs results in an accumulation of norepinephrine, serotonin, and dopamine within nerve terminals. The relief of symptoms of depression is a result of the increased production and accumulation of these neurotransmitters. On the other hand, scientists have discovered that drugs which produce symptoms of severe depression in patients interfere with the capacity of nerve endings to store neurotransmitter substances.

In general, behavioral studies and clinical findings are compatible with the idea that neurotransmitters are involved in mood, with deficiencies producing depression and overproduction likely resulting in euphoria.

The findings concerning lowered levels of neurotransmitters in depressed subjects take on added significance when one considers the various means by which neurotransmitter production can be increased. A basic premise of *The Emotional Maintenance Manual* plan is that through daily activity and diet you can increase your production of neurohormones which affect mood and can thereby increase your chances of coping with stressful situations. Certainly you should be willing to give yourself the advantage which biochemical research has now offered.

Maintaining your body aids enormously in reaching a high level of emotional stability. Mind-body harmony is a cornerstone of the Manual's theory. Or, as the ancient Romans put it:

*Mens sana in machina sana.**

* A healthy mind in a healthy vehicle.

Day 2

7:00 A.M.: Breathe oxygen immediately upon arising and then place Affirmation Card 3, FIND, in a prominent place. Again, consider the meaning of the card in its relationship to your life. Think of synonyms like expose, locate, discover, come upon; what thoughts and feelings do they release? Is FIND a happy word for you? Think of times FIND has brought satisfaction—finding a treasured item—or sadness—discovering that you had lost someone you once loved. Remember, the purpose of this exercise is to put you in touch with your feelings, to teach you to recognize and pay attention to them.

7:05 A.M.: Relax to whatever sound is pleasing to you. Continue to think about the word FIND.

7:15 A.M.: Perform the toe-touching and stretching exercises described in Day 1.

7:30 A.M.: Dress for exercise.

7:40 A.M.: Jogging, walking, roving, bicycling, or swimming. Bring your whistle.

8:10 A.M.: Shower—you may substitute a hot bath or jacuzzi.

8:45 A.M.: Breakfast: fruit or juice, banana, bran, brewer's yeast, honey and milk, and your vitamins. Think about FIND.

9:30 A.M.: Travel Log: Snapshots.

Read over the thoughts you recorded yesterday in the Journey Plan notebook of your Travel Log. Now, in the notebook you have entitled Snapshots, you will amplify and clarify these thoughts pertaining to the present moment of your life.

In Snapshots, you will be reviewing the present period of your life from another, nonrational perspective. You will be seeing the emotional after-images of events and recording them. Since this very internalized sort of perception is infrequently used by most people in our society, it may be necessary for you to redevelop these skills. When you learn to establish an atmosphere that makes it possible for attention to be turned inward, these capacities should manifest themselves in an active and strong way.

The title Snapshots describes the symbolic nature of these internalized perceptions. Your images may be visual or may center in any of the other senses. You may recall the memory of an aroma, a sound or a physical sensation.

Most important, do not consciously or deliberately create or choose these perceptions. Rather, quietly and passively allow them to appear in whatever form and in whatever sensory aspect they choose. With your attention turned inward, you will observe them as though they were dreams.

It is a good idea to place your Journey Plan entry in front of you while recording perceptions in Snapshots. After reading the Journey Plan material, sit quietly with your eyes closed. Feel the tone and quality of the period you described in the Journey Plan. Don't think about the events of the period, don't evaluate or make judgments about them. Instead, allow images to form: see them, smell them, hear them, intuit them, feel them.

These perceptions may first come as stirrings in your body, as joyous surges or as stomach knots. Whatever form they take, observe them neutrally and record them in your Snapshots notebook.

10:30 A.M.:   Spend the next one and a half hours *playing*. Leave the house, bring your whistle and your affirmation word. Just enjoy yourself. Don't do anything structured, and above all, don't feel guilty because you aren't. Follow your urges. Look at faces while walking in your neighborhood, or take an aimless drive in your car. Play with a child—your own or a friend's. Don't organize games, just let things happen. Children know all about this; you can follow your pal's cue.

This exercise helps you remember what it's like just to feel good—because you deserve to. It is a way to clean out those dark corners of your mind; it is something you should do periodically, with purpose. Play is NOT a cut-throat game of tennis; it is not a poker game with the boys; it is not the dinner party for eight that you're giving Saturday. It's not sitting in front of the TV set or even reading a good book. It should be a conscious act of putting aside some time to do nothing but enjoy yourself, with the emphasis on the second word!

12:00 **noon:**   Have lunch at the restaurant of your choice. Select from the menu foods from the list on pages 138–140.

After dining, concentrate on eliciting a positive reaction from another person. As you enjoy the atmosphere of the restaurant or, if you prefer, as you stroll around on the side-walk outside, pay someone a compliment, smile at them, do something good for someone. Be as bold as you dare. Don't be afraid of rejection. After all, it's those strangers out there who really need a friend.

1:30–2:00 P.M.:   Relaxation exercises. Follow the procedure outlined on Day 1.

2:00–3:00 P.M.:   Mood Clinic

Bring your Mood Clinic into being. Close your eyes and concentrate on re-creating the workshop exactly as you did yesterday. You will now use the workshop to review past actions and plan for the future. Relax in your chair and bring your Mood Clinic screen into focus. Turn back your calendar and visualize a time when you were very depressed. See yourself in a particular place—maybe you were on a bus, or maybe you were sitting alone in your room, late on a hot summer night. Refer to your books: were you ill at the time? Were your finances at an all-time low? Remember how you felt; for the moment let that awful, numbing feeling permeate your being. Now, try to remember what you did or did not do to bring yourself out of it. Did you do nothing, did you just passively wait for it to pass? Did you immerse yourself in activity? Was it productive, or destructive? Did you blame others? Make a mental list of four or five courses of action you took. What was the outcome? See yourself some time later. Are you pleased with the results? Most probably, looking back you will realize that there was a lot you could have done for yourself but didn't.

An antidepression list follows. Re-create that depressed state and utilize these preventive, curative steps, in conjunction with the material of your own past life—your friends, your activities, your surroundings.

1. Create order in your life. Do the things you've always done, maintain regular habits. Reflect on these small accomplishments; they will make you feel more worthy and competent.

2. Keep up appearances. Letting yourself and your living quarters fall apart only strengthens the idea that there's nothing to look good for.

3. Don't give up a project: you have to make things in your life matter.

4. Don't suppress anger. Resigning yourself to mistreatment makes you believe that you deserve it, and that you'll always get it. There is a deadly calm in depression. Take every opportunity to feel strongly and act on your feelings.

5. Study and learn something new each day. It gives you the sense that there is something new, and better, in the future.

6. Stop talking about your problems for a specific period. Talk can perpetuate them, and make you feel that you have nothing else to offer.

7. Get yourself a pet: the give and take will force you to be part of life.

8. Take note of the good moments in your life, especially the unexpected ones. Open yourself to all pleasurable events.

9. Spend time with people who are energetic and hopeful. Their optimism might be annoying and childish, and their energy might seem a rebuke to you, but their presence is challenging and will force you to look at your own harmful choices.

You have just completed a cognitive exercise in reverse. At some future time, or maybe even now, you will have to do a *real* run-through on possible courses of action when you are in the midst of a depressive state. Use this list in your Mood Clinic when that situation arises, take these steps, and deal with your depressions from now on in an efficient, intelligent, constructive way.

A second Mood Clinic exercise is learning to deal with injunctions: rules, *dicta,* handed down from parents, lovers, mates—anyone close. For example: "If you don't listen to me, you'll never make it," or "Unless you help out more, you're going to wind up going through life alone." If we hear these injunctions often enough, we start to live by them, and because they are negatively based, we look for situations that will provide the same negative reinforcement in our lives.

Think of an injunction that was imposed on you some time ago: it might take a while, because if it did its job, you have, without thinking about it, incorporated it into your life. You might have to go back to your childhood; bring yourself onto your screen as you were at twelve or fourteen. If you can't remember an exact instance, create one with the equipment in your Mood Clinic. As long as you mirror the substance of the situation—your mother nagging about your laziness in a particular way, or your father about your cigarette smoking—you can create a situation that will bring forth the emotions that are part of you now.

Now flip your calendar forward: what part of you is still living by that injunction? Do you feel guilty at some level every time you don't make your bed? Or, more seriously, have you incorporated the feeling that you are never going to amount to anything because you don't "give" enough in a relationship?

Now use your Mood Clinic screen to visualize actual situations in which these injunctions affected you—a relationship that failed, or the job that never worked out. Imagine yourself free of the particular, harmful injunction, and act out a different ending for each situation. Concentrate on the feeling of freedom you now have, and remember the injunction that has been your burden. Every time you feel it creeping into your life, deflect it. Give yourself positive strokes when you accomplish something good, whether minor or important, rather than reinforcing the negative behavior these injunctions have created. Use positive reinforcement to free yourself from old, debilitating patterns.

3:30 P.M.:   An experiment in self-awareness.

The following exercise is a guide for personal growth. It will give you an idea of who you are by evaluating where you've come from and where you're going. It is not a personality test or diagnostic evaluation. Its intent is to make you aware of your own development.*

1. Circle five words below that best describe your mother:

Warm	Worrier	Friendly	Talkative
Dictatorial	Bored	Pessimistic	Silent
Sullen	Angry	Silly	Nagging
Gay	Rational	Gloomy	Dumb
Calm	Optimistic	Outgoing	Punctual
Sarcastic	Depressed	Critical	Loving
Perfectionist	Successful	Withdrawn	Failure
Happy	Martyr	Insecure	Stingy
Emotional	Cold	Sexy	Demanding
Tolerant	Impatient	Nervous	Crazy

2. Now underline the five words that best describe your father.

3. Which underlined or circled words describe your relationships with others?

4. When you were a child and your parents or someone else criticized you, how did you feel? (underline)

Angry	Sad	Rejected	Unloved
Picked on	Guilty	Tearful	Frustrated
Deserving	Ambivalent	Afraid	Hopeless

5. What are your feelings now when someone criticizes you? _____

_____

_____

_____

6. How did you usually feel when people praised you?

* This exercise was adapted in part from *A Winner's Workbook*, 1977, Price, Stern & Sloane.

Excited	Deserving	Warm	Ambivalent
Bored	Loved	Puzzled	Angry
Manipulated	Worthwhile	Embarrassed	

7. What did you have to do to elicit the feelings indicated above? _____

_____

_____

_____

8. How do you rate yourself in making nonemotional decisions?

Very Low	Low		Average	Above Average	Very High
0	1	2	3	4	5	6	7	8

9. Using the same scale, how do you rate in comparison with those listed below?

Other people in general ( )   Your spouse ( )
A few friends ( )   Your boss ( )
Your children ( )   Your fellow employees ( )

10. Which phrase best describes how you handle problems or make decisions?

Get away from _____   Get on with _____
Get nowhere with _____   Get rid of _____

11. Which of the following games are most familiar to you? (underline):

Ain't It Awful.
Gee, You're a Wonderful Boss.
If It Weren't for Them.
I'm Only Trying to Help.
Harried—I rush, rush, rush to feel important and some day I'll collapse.
Courtroom—Everyone knows you're wrong and I'm right.

Sunny Side Up—I'm seeing the world through rose-colored glasses.

Waiting for Social Security—Some day my ship will come in.

Uproar—I'm the greatest. You're stupid.

Corner—Damned if I do and damned if I don't.

Mine's Better Than Yours.

Poor Little Me.

Look How Hard I Try.

Kick Me

12. What were some of the DO messages your parents gave you? _____

_____

_____

_____

_____

13. What were some of the DON'T messages your parents gave you? _____

_____

_____

_____

_____

14. What were your early childhood projections about grown-up life? _____

_____

_____

_____

15. Finish the following sentences:
Someday I'll retire and then _____

_____

_____

_____

Someday I'll get promoted and then

_____

_____

_____

Someday I'll go back to school and then

_____

_____

_____

Someday the kids will be raised and then

_____

_____

_____

Someday I'll win the Irish Sweepstakes and then

_____

_____

_____

This exercise should clarify some injunctions that influence your development. Go back and take a look at all fifteen areas. Interpret your developmental profile. From awareness comes understanding and from understanding comes change.

3:30 P.M.:   Change to Affirmation Card four, CARE, and spend a few moments considering what this card means to you. What is CARE? It is nurturing, looking after someone or something dependent on you—a child, a lover, a pet, a plant. It is putting yourself in someone else's perspective, entering their dimension. "*Care*" comes from the same Latin root as *cure*. Care heals. When you say, "I care about him," that means "He matters to me." That investment of yourself in another enriches the both of you. How do you show care? Who cares for you, and how do they show it?

3:45 P.M.:   Exercise: bicycling, swimming, jogging or roving. Continue to think about CARE as you exercise.

4:30 P.M.:   A. Pay a short visit to someone you haven't seen in the last few weeks. You might explain the purpose of the visit as an effort to renew an old friendship. Or

B. Give yourself permission to do something you have always been afraid to do. Bring your whistle!

6:00 P.M.:   Dinner. Have a light dinner of salad, wheat germ, vegetables, fruit, and dessert. Think about CARE.

6:45 P.M.:   Replacing the Old Scripts of Your Life with New Goals.

One of the purposes of the EMM 3-Day Crash Program is to help you determine realistic and attainable goals for your life. Upon completion of the Program, you will be drawing up a contract with yourself, a promise to work toward a major goal. The following exercise is practice for that commitment.

Everyone must, at one time or another, decide whether to drift aimlessly through life or assume responsibility for the future. Responsibility for one's future means *making rational decisions in the pursuit of realistic goals.*

Attainment of ambitious goals can be difficult; obstacles abound. Examine your past: you will recall attitudes or modes of thought that stunted the development of goal-oriented behavior. One of the most common is fear of the unknown. Remember, at any given moment you must be able to give up what you are for what you could become. Procrastination, discounting, lack of self-confidence, rationalization, and unrealistic thinking are some other stumbling blocks that people themselves create to keep them from realizing their goals.

In order to attain your goal, whatever it may be, it is necessary to break it down into small, specific steps. The secret of goal attainment is the willingness to plan and the courage to pursue in the face of hardship.

In this exercise, select an easily attainable goal for yourself. Your goal may be to reduce tension and anxiety when you drive; to get your building superintendent to fix that leaking faucet; or to learn to cook a three-course meal so you can have dinner guests. Write it down and follow it with the sequence of steps needed for completion. Make sure that the first step is immediately attainable, and make the steps progressively more difficult. However, you must be able to achieve your goal within the next few days. For example, if you've decided to ask a neighbor to replace some bushes his gardener accidentally cut down, your first step might be to call a wholesale nursery and price various sizes of the bush, and list those with the address and phone number of the nursery. Your second step might be to get out your property map and prove that the bushes were on your land. Your third step, now that you are prepared, would be to pay a visit to your neighbor. And so forth, until you have gotten what you wanted: what is rightfully yours.

By writing out a sequence of steps for attaining your goal, you will have formulated a plan of action. If you have not acted upon your plan in twenty-four hours, you will know that the sequence of steps was not broken down into its simplest form. Revise your plan, if this is the case, and take that first step. Post your plan in a conspicuous place so that you can continue to monitor your program.

7:00 P.M.:   Spend the evening on one of the following leisurely activities:
 1. reading a novel
 2. painting or drawing
 3. a hobby

10:15 P.M.:   Record the events of the day and your feelings about them in your Daily Log. Follow the same format you used yesterday.

11:00 P.M.:   Breathe oxygen. Take a glass of skim milk. Sleep well!

Day 3

7:00 A.M.: Wake up and breathe oxygen. Place Affirmation Card 5, TRUST, in a prominent spot. Reflect on the word: are you a trustful person? Were you once, and did something make you change? Does that make you angry or sad? Does someone trust you? Did you ever betray that trust? How did it make you feel? Think of who and how you trust: a lover, an inanimate object like your car, your child.

7:05 A.M.: Relax to the sound of music of your choice.

7:15 A.M.: Stretching exercises.

7:30 A.M.: Dress for exercise.

7:40 A.M.: Jogging, roving, bicycling, or swimming. Bring your whistle, and think about TRUST.

8:10 A.M.: Shower or jacuzzi.

8:45 A.M.: Breakfast: fruit or juice, banana, bran, brewer's yeast, honey, milk, and your vitamins.

9:30 A.M.: Travel Log.
    Today's diary work is to be done in the notebook entitled Intersections: Roads Taken and Not Taken. This sec-

tion of the Travel Log allows you to return to those times that were points of transition, intersections in your life, where a change of some kind became inevitable.

Some of those changes took place because of decisions you yourself made. Others occurred as a result of decisions made by others, or were forced upon you by the impersonal circumstances of life. However they happened, they were singular experiences which determined the direction and shaped the content of your life from that point onward.

As you now consider your life in retrospect, you will recognize that the choices you made necessarily left many possibilities untouched and unexplored. Intersections is the vehicle through which you may discover and consider those possibilities.

Think back to the important intersections in your own life. Your choice of school, career, a marriage partner, only represent a few. Carefully recollect and write down as many of these important choices as possible. Leave several lines in your notebook under each intersection.

Consider the choice you actually made in each case and write down how it has now affected your life. Then consider the alternatives available to you at the time you made a decision and write down what effect each of these would have had on your life, had you chosen it instead.

The potential within you, which these alternatives represent, was not able to find an avenue of expression at an earlier time, but may be at a further stage of development now. When you first felt it necessary to reject some or all of these possibilities, they may have been premature intimations of capacities or talents which were present but needed more time to mature. Or perhaps the external situation was not favorable at that time. By recalling these experiences you can reacquaint yourself with that potential that has not yet been expressed. By traveling back to the various intersections of your life, you may discover that alternatives rejected in the past are now both possible and desirable for you. Some of the roads you did not take may now be seen as starting points for future development.

10:30 A.M.: Language: Symbols and Communication.

Think about language: emotional language, rational language, devious language, unspoken language. Whatever form it takes, language is an attempt to share the content of the experience going on within us; all we can ever really share, however, are the symbols of that experience.

Language's function is not just the transmission of ideas: it is designed to obtain emotional results more often than rational ones, and to alter conditions within ourselves rather than in others. On a sheet of paper, list examples of the following sort of language, and think about how you use them.

1. Language to express emotion about yourself. (I feel happy. Content.)
2. Language spoken just to drown out the silence. (How are you? You are looking well. Flatter-chatter.)
3. Language spoken for its own beauty. (Clouds of crowded daffodils.)
4. Language as poetry and song to establish belonging. (I need you. There is a small hotel with a wishing well. I wish we were there together.)
5. Language that establishes relationships. (I love you. You are my friend. I care about you.)
6. Language that affects others' emotions. (You rotten son of a bitch. I think you have extraordinary charm.)
7. Language to affect others' behavior. (Stop that.)
8. Language to express insights—philosophical language. (I have just discovered the newness of you. I think, therefore I am.)
9. Language that communicates ideas and facts. (Two plus two equals four. Advertising, graphics.)
10. Language that has word-magic; in which the words are loaded with more effect than in ordinary usage. (Once upon a time there was a beautiful princess.)

Words are imbued with tremendous meaning—large words, small words, words left unsaid, words that hurt, silent words. Some words cost us nothing; others are very expensive. We often use words incorrectly and cause misunderstanding and pain. Words are a way of knowing what we sometimes feel for others and ourselves. Write down five words describing one person who has meant a lot to you.

This exercise will help you become more aware of the importance of language. Think about the words you use during the next few days. Can you be more expressive, more concise?

11:30 A.M.:   Developing a New Image of Yourself.

Have you ever really thought about the kind of person you would like to be? We all think things like (take your choice): "I'd like to be rich, with houses, yachts, Lear jets, a wonderful lifetime mate, every man/woman in the world in love with me, perfect children, fame, personal success, immortality." But those aren't realistic goals for 99.99 percent of us, and what's more to the point, you can have all of those feathers in your cap and still be miserable—it has happened. What we're talking about here is much more basic and realistic: what sort of *person* would you like to be?

On a blank sheet of paper, write a paragraph evisioning your new self: "I am thinner, with very good muscle tone; my health is terrific. I am more content with life, and I don't blame others for its hard knocks. I am not afraid to express my opinions, even at the risk of starting an argument at a very formal dinner party; I know I will feel better about myself if I do. People will recognize me for what I am; I will no longer fade into the background. I will become _____, changing my job, and this time I will really focus on and learn my work, becoming more aggressive and less self-abnegating. I will rise to the top of my profession." Or, to show how different people's aspirations can be: "I will learn to be lovable, so that someone can love me. I will be healthy because of it, and my headaches and stomach aches will cease. I will be married and have a child, possibly. I will leave my profession, which will be a shock to everyone because I am seemingly so immersed in it, and I will become a _____. I will make a lot of money, because I am tough. But most of all I would like to love and be loved."

After you have completed outlining your new self-image, reflect upon how comfortable you now feel in that role. What are your emotions? Are you satisfied with your new position? How does the change effect your relationships with friends, with family? Record your answers to these and other questions you may have concerning your degree of security in your new role.

11:55 A.M.: Have you taken Step 1 toward the goal you set for yourself yesterday?

12:00 noon: Stop off for a relaxing lunch. Bring your whistle—have you had to use it yet? Lunch should again include foods from your acceptable list.

After the meal, you will again do something positive for another person. As you lunch, consider the possibilities. Think of something you have wanted to do for a long time but just haven't been able to muster up the courage for. Plan your deed carefully, then follow through. Don't forget your affirmation word.

After you have completed your activity, stop and purchase a small gift for yourself.

1:45 P.M.: Actualizing exercise.
With a set of crayons, express these feelings in color: love, hate, fear, jealousy, anger, stress, guilt, joy, sadness, calm.

What color represents love? What color represents stress, guilt? Now turn to the Emotional Wheel and color in each area. Visualize the color of the emotion. Is it vivid and bright, or soft and pastel? Color the emotion. Feel it. Remember it.

After you've done this, take a look at it. Examine the

THE EMOTIONAL WHEEL

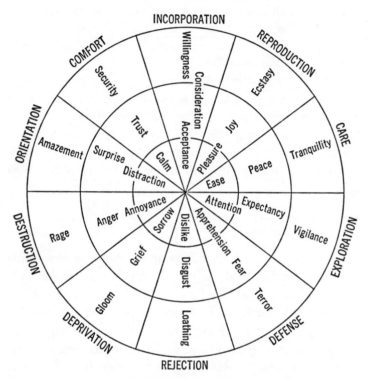

Emotions are barometers of feelings; counterpoints to our motives and behavior. In 1880, William James assumed that bodily changes such as rapid breathing and perspiration were directly stimulated by fear. Emotion, he reported, is nothing more than our awareness of bodily changes as they take place. Since James' initial theories, there has been subsequent investigation of the hypothesis that emotions themselves determine bodily changes and vice versa.

On the emotional wheel, emotions are organized by similarity, intensity, and polarity. Emotions next to each other in the circle are far apart. In fact, emotions that are opposites in the circle are opposites in life. Within the circle, the farther an emotion is toward the edge, the more intense it is. Thus, rage is more intense an emotion than anger, which is more intense than annoyance. This circle helps us to understand the meaning and degree of our emotionality.

color and the art and re-experience the feelings that you have expressed.

2:00 P.M.: Mood Clinic Exercises.

Bring your Mood Clinic Workshop into being exactly as you did yesterday. Have your tape recorder handy. Relax and concentrate.

Using your screen, imagine any problem situation you have encountered over the last three days. Go back farther, if you have to; but it should be recent enough to be a) unresolved, or b) for you to still be feeling its effects. Any situation that has resulted in an emotional response of sadness, fear, hate, or anger is appropriate (don't forget telephone encounters). And you should not be pleased with your reactions and actions within the situation. If you think you acted intelligently, constructively, concisely, clearly, then choose another situation.

Describe what you perceive on the screen into the tape recorder. Be as detailed as possible, include the people involved and their actions and reactions, as well as yours.

After you have re-enacted the scene mentally and recorded it, imagine handling the same situation in a different and positive way. Try these strategies where they apply: This time I won't shout and get so angry that I a) leave, or b) can't think straight. This time I won't interrupt; I'll hear her out. This time I won't change the subject, or criticize when I'm criticized. This time I won't blame her because I know it was a) my fault, or b) at least partly my fault. This time I will say what I really mean; I'll be frank. This time I won't tolerate his threats and modify what I'm saying because I'm afraid of him/her. This time I'll try to reach a satisfactory solution for both/all of us instead of trying to win; trying to be the victim; trying to smooth things over temporarily; trying to destroy him/her.

As you visualize your alternate behavior, also imagine what the reactions of the others would be. Again, make a detailed description of these activities into the tape recorder.

Continue using the screen and the tape recorder for as many problem situations as you can recall over the last three days. For each situation, first visualize and describe what really happened, then visualize and describe what might have happened in the same situation. Then listen to the recording and think about what you've discovered about yourself and your behavior.

3:00 P.M.: Replace your morning Affirmation Card with your final card, LOVE.

An overused word, "love" slides off our tongues often and without thought to its real meaning, or the demands real love makes of us. What does LOVE really mean to you? The shared ecstasy with a lover that we all seek, that is brilliant but often short-lived? Or the intense need that you felt for your parents, when you were small, or that equally intense desire to protect and care for your child? Is it the selfless giving, drudgery and sadness of caring for a family member who is ill? Yearning, life-enhancing ecstasy, need, endless giving: think about what LOVE really means to you.

3:15 P.M.: Visit someone you know who is currently experiencing emotional duress as a result of extenuating circumstances, either financial, family, or social matters. During your visit concentrate on understanding the underlying reasons for this person's reactions and offer only sincere words of encouragement.

4:30 P.M.: Afternoon exercise: jogging, roving, bicycling, swimming. You may substitute tennis, racquetball, etc., if you have a partner. Bring your whistle.

5:00 P.M.: Have you completed another step toward the goal you set yesterday? Take the time to do it now.

5:30 P.M.: Follow the relaxation routine described for the same time period on Day 1.

6:00 P.M.: Dinner: salad, fruit, and a milk protein drink

including wheat germ. Remember LOVE.

7:00 P.M.: On the final evening of the 3-Day Crash Program, we encourage you to entertain yourself. You may want to go to a movie, a concert, dancing, or you may be more inclined to relax at home with a good book or a special hobby. Whatever your choice, it should be a reward, from you to you. Enjoy your current high energy level.

10:15 P.M.: Enter your activities and thoughts for the day in the Daily Log. Before going to sleep, play back the tape you recorded earlier during the Mood Clinic sessions. Set your alarm to wake up an hour earlier tomorrow morning, and in that hour read the following chapter.

11:00–11:30 P.M.: Breathe oxygen. Sleep.

The Contract

One final exercise will assist you in reinforcing the positive things you have learned about yourself in the last three days. It is a behavioral contract, drawn up by you and for you, establishing the objective criteria needed for attainment of a major goal of your choice. The goal should be on the level of: increasing assertiveness, becoming more productive, increasing creativity, communicating better with others, making new friends. Remember the exercise you started on Day 2? The first step of your major goal should be attainable in the near future—no longer than a week. Reaching it will give you a sense of accomplishment that will spur you on to more difficult steps.

Complete the following contract now and post it in a conspicuous but private place in your office, study, or bedroom. Once it is honored and completed, you will make another.

Every year, draw up a contract with yourself to accomplish specific goals.

Based on my current desires, expectations and needs, I have resolved to alter my life. I have established for myself a major goal and will strive to reach that goal. (At any given moment I must be able to give up what I am for what I could become.) My major goal is: _____

_____

I expect to reach this goal on or about (date) _____
Realizing that my major goal will require a planned sequence of action, I have established for myself a series of smaller goals. The first step in attaining my major goal is _____

_____

_____

to be accomplished by (date) _____
The second step in attaining my major goal is _____

_____

_____

to be accomplished by (date) _____
The third step in attaining my major goal is _____

_____

_____

to be accomplished by (date) _____
The fourth step in attaining my major goal is _____

_____

_____

to be accomplished by (date) _____

The fifth step in attaining my major goal is _____

_____

_____

Signed _____   Date _____

PART III

The EMM Life-Long Maintenance Program

Your Weekly Investment

You're probably asking "What happens now? What do I do with the rest of my life?"

Participation in the 3-Day Crash Program will have increased your energy level, your awareness of your own and others' motivations, and your self-confidence. Most importantly, you are now at the starting point on the road to emotional stability and have clear-cut directions on how to travel that road.

But it is a well-known fact that the benefits of a therapy session with a psychiatrist last at most 72 hours; similarly you will experience a general high lasting a couple of weeks after finishing the Program as a natural result of the emotional and physical work you have done on yourself.

Now you must outline a weekly schedule that will, if you follow it, keep you on the track on a daily basis and monitor your lifelong progress. No psychiatrist could ever do this much for you, even if he stayed by your side day and night. Only you can do it, and we are going to show you how.

You will be asked to turn over five hours out of a weekly

168 hours to the Lifelong Maintenance Program. During those five hours you will exercise your body and your self-awareness. You will also be provided with a sensible diet that will help regulate your emotional well-being. You will be given guidelines on how to monitor and adjust your environment, both external and internal, and your biochemistry through exercise and diet. It is a program geared to take care of the *whole you*. Many elements will be familiar to you, as they have been drawn from the 3-Day Crash Program.

Five hours is a small investment to make when you consider the benefits you'll receive as a result of the program. Steal an hour or two from TV, and a half-hour of commuting time two or three times a week.

Weekly Checklist—Lifelong Maintenance Program

Exercise	forty-five minutes three times a week	
		= 2 hours and 15 minutes
	(See the recommended exercises on pages 112–121)	
Diet*		
Relaxation	five minutes every day =	35 minutes
Daily Log	fifteen minutes a day =	1 hour and 45 minutes
Occasional	exercises, prescriptions, tests as needed, twenty-five minutes a week =	25 minutes
	TOTAL	5 hours

The exercises you perform can be an extension of those you did for the Crash Program—roving, swimming, jogging, bicycling, tennis, racquetball, situps in place—in short, anything that increases your pulse rate. A chapter on exercise fol-

---

* Your diet, of course, is an integral part of the LMP, but it takes no more time to follow our plan than it does to eat a candy bar.

lows—read it and follow it as if your life depends on it—it does.

The relaxation routines you learned should be performed for five minutes every day. Choose your time—when you get up, when you get home from work, behind the closed door of your office at lunch time. Remember these five minutes a day—they are worth their weight in gold, because they serve to keep you in touch with your emotions.

Good nutrition, as you know by now, is essential not only for your physical health but also your emotional well-being. The chapter in this section on nutrition contains the EMM diet and explains why the EMM emphasizes specific foods. It offers a lot of latitude, but be sure to follow it.

The Travel Log and Mood Clinic exercises can be used less regularly—whenever the need arises. The Mood Clinic will be especially useful in times of emotional stress when you want to review fully the components of a particular situation. Be sure to use it at least once a month regardless of need in order to keep in practice.

Recording your thoughts and feelings in your Daily Log will give you objectivity and distance from them and help you make clearer decisions. It is a discipline you can establish by setting aside the same fifteen minutes every day.

You will want to renew your contract every six months. Use the same form each time. Your new contract can be an extension of the old one—for example, you may have become more assertive with your friends, but now wish to increase your assertiveness on the job—or it can go off in a new direction.

When you have finished reading this chapter, test yourself again on the Emotional Maintenance Inventory and note the difference in your score. It will probably show only slight overall improvement since some of the scales measure attitudes, feelings, and habits over a period of months. Test yourself on the Inventory every six months and chart your progress. If your score begins to rise it may be necessary to repeat the 3-Day Crash Program. However, if you adhere to your Life-long Maintenance Program, in all likelihood your Inventory score will show a healthy, steady decline.

Part Four of the EMM is your Manual for Maximum Performance. It includes an 8-Point Tune-up Checklist, and chapters devoted to specific problem areas, like relationships, depression, and conflict. Each chapter contains *RX Prescriptions*—emotional medicine that you can prescribe for yourself. It is very important that you follow through on these prescriptions, that you actualize your cure.

You are also encouraged to write your own RX's; it will help especially when you are depressed. As part of your regular LMP, buy yourself a 3″ × 5″ pad, write "RX" on the cover, and keep it with the Manual. When you need it, take it out and be your own doctor. To start you in the right direction, write prescriptions like:

1. Do something; get out of the house. Change a negative thought into a positive activity.
2. Look for something positive in the first person you see and tell him about it.
3. Praise yourself. Choose a positive attribute and repeat it out loud to yourself.

Don't cheat; don't merely verbalize your prescription; write it down. Make it work for you.

The final guide for lifelong emotional health is the Emotional Checklist. Read what follows carefully and incorporate it into your life.

Emotional Checklist

Every time you face an emotional problem, make it your business to run through the following list, much as you would read the indicators and dials on your car's instrument panel if it starts to choke and sputter going up a hill.

1. *Do you have enough fuel* to enter into this situation? Do you have—or is it worth—the energy, the time, the ability, the motivation and desire to see it through to a satisfactory conclusion? Will you or can you give it your honest, straightforward attention?

2. *Examine the problem:* How deep is your involvement? Someone else's? How is it similar or different from other situations. What are its components—for example, are you depressed because you are angry? Are you anxious because you are in a situation that always causes you anxiety? Analyze; break the problem down into its parts.

3. *Define the problem:* Now that you have broken it down, gather together all aspects of the problem. Look for its essence, give it a name. "I am *angry,* this anger saps my energy and I want to be calm and content." Clarify your goals.

4. *List possible solutions:* Don't be lazy—think of as many as you can, even ones you consider outrageous. Bringing them into being can lead you down productive paths you have never traveled, and they can always be modified or dropped later.

5. *Determine the best solution:* What is the solution that is most beneficial and least destructive? Most economical? Most direct? Of greatest duration?

6. *Act:* None of the above steps gains meaning until you make them a reality. By the same token, acting on impulse, without information, is most often as unproductive as not acting at all.

7. *Review:* Look back on all the steps you took: were your decisions accurate? Could they have been better? Compare the outcome to your input in terms of quality and quantity. In this way you will be better prepared for your next emotional problem-solving experience. *Informed* experience is the best teacher!

For now, today, be proud of your accomplishment. You have completed and just started a rigorous program of life change. Graduate yourself—and celebrate your commencement. Take a friend to dinner tonight. Share your bright, shining new self with those who are close to you—the you who has stepped out from behind hazily expressed desires and inappropriate emotions to look at yourself and the rest of the world squarely in the face, with less fear, anger, depression, confusion, than you thought possible. It feels good, doesn't it?

A Menu for Healthier Life

Are you 15 percent or more overweight?
Do you eat meat several times a day?
Do you smoke?
Do you exercise only occasionally?
Do you drink more than 4 ounces of liquor or half a bottle of wine or several quarts of beer each day?
Is your blood pressure high? Cholesterol up?
Do you take tranquilizers or pills to calm you down or to pep you up?

If you answer YES to most of these questions, your chances of living to age 50 is less than 50 percent. If you want to live longer and feel healthier, you must:

Reach a normal weight for your size and frame.
Eat meat not more than 4 times a week.
Give up smoking.
Exercise as though your life depended on it.
Moderate your drinking.
Lower your blood pressure to normal; reduce your cholesterol level through supervised diet.
Be very moderate with any tranquilizers.
Sleep 8 hours a night.
Have a breakfast, a proper lunch, and a light dinner.

The exercise and nutritional programs outlined in the following chapters will help you achieve these goals. Read the material carefully and then make it a part of your life. The rewards are immeasurable.

Exercise

In the last ten years or so, we have become enormously health conscious. The reasons are varied and numerous: an increased awareness of the negative effects of our rich diets and sedentary lifestyles; friends dying of heart disease at too early an age; more leisure time; the growing trend toward inner-directed activities.

But whatever the cause, acting to preserve your health is one of the best investments you will ever make. These are some of the reasons why exercise and fitness are of value even when the physical demands of living are minimal.

1. Strength and endurance developed through regular exercise enable you to perform daily tasks with relative ease. You use only a small part of your physical reserve in routine activity.
2. Skill and agility gained through practice provide for economy of movement. This is another factor in minimizing physical effort required for routine tasks.
3. Poise and grace are by-products of efficient movement.

They help you to feel at ease in social situations and are factors in good appearance.

4. Good muscle tone and posture can protect you from certain back problems caused by sedentary living.

5. Controlling your weight is mostly a matter of balancing your food intake with your exercise output. Inactivity is often as critical as overeating in creeping overweight.

6. To the degree that physical activity helps control your weight, it will also aid in preventing degenerative diseases. Diseases of the heart and blood vessels, diabetes, and arthritis strike the obese more often and more seriously than they strike those of desirable weight.

7. Mounting evidence indicates that exercise is one of the factors in maintaining the health of the heart and blood vessels. Active people have fewer heart attacks and a better recovery rate from such attacks than the inactive.

8. Enjoyable exercise can provide relief from tension and serve as a safe and natural tranquilizer.

9. Feeling physically fit helps you to build a desirable self-concept. You need to see yourself at your optimum physically as well as in other ways.

10. Dynamic fitness can help to protect you against accidents and may be a lifesaving factor in emergencies. Reacting quickly and with physical decisiveness may enable you to avert a serious accident.

You're probably aware of most of these reasons already. But what most people don't know—and marathon runners know in a hazy sort of way—is that this same sort of exercise is therapy for emotional illness. We aren't just talking here about "feeling exhausted but wonderful." There is biochemical proof that sustained, regular, oxygenating exercise also speeds up production of the two important neurotransmitters, norepinephrine and serotonin. What serious runners feel, over and above physical exertion, is an actual "high." A few years ago, we might have thought they were just "communing with nature" or "getting in touch with" their bodies, but we now have scientific support. Sustained aerobic exercise activates the adrenal glands which in turn release adrenaline, the precursor of the neurotransmitters, which are natural antidepressants and tranquilizers.

What sort of exercise should you adopt for your Lifelong Maintenance Program? We listed a choice of several for the 3-Day Crash Program: jogging, roving, swimming, and bicycling. The advantages and disadvantages of each are discussed below.

Jogging:

Probably the most popular of the aerobic-oxygenating exercises, it has taken the country by storm. Marathon races have cropped up in many major cities, and the old, established ones, like the Boston Marathon, are thronged, not just by spectators, but by participants. Why? Running builds cardiovascular endurance, capacity, and elasticity faster and more dramatically than any other exercise. It is also, with roving, the least complicated method. It requires almost no equipment, can be done anywhere—even in front of your TV set—and costs almost nothing. You don't need a sweatsuit, you just need the correct shoes. Just open your front door and go— uphill, on level ground, around a track, across a field, along the beach, down to Wall Street and back, alone, with your lover, or your dog. There are some drawbacks however: it requires a great deal of stamina and if you are not in good shape, have recently been ill, or are getting on in years without having exercised regularly, it is not wise to start your exercise program with jogging. You might however want to graduate to it later. Jogging can also cause back problems as well as foot and shin injuries and swellings because of the constant shock and compression when you come down on a sprint. For this reason, it is important to have well-cushioned, supportive shoes. Never jog barefoot, even if you're only jogging in place in front of your TV set.

Roving:

This is a combination of walking and running, and you decide if and when to switch your pace. Distance, not time, is the important consideration; you are not racing. Set your own pace to complete your target distance; how you complete it is entirely up to you. There is no pressure to run a mile in seven minutes. Because you are exercising less strenuously, of course, you won't get results as fast as you will by jogging. But on the other hand, if you are in poor physical shape and the whole idea of *running* for *miles* terrifies you, start out by roving. Smell the air, notice your surroundings, enjoy your healthy new body, and you will probably find yourself exuberantly bursting into a run more often than not in the near future.

Swimming:

This means doing laps, of course. You do need a lake, ocean, or pool, which is a setback for many of us who live in cold climates. But you can join a Y or a health club, especially if you live in a big city. Swimming is the preferred aerobic exercise for many people. It exercises the entire body evenly, toning all your muscles as you fight the extra resistance that water offers. It is not damaging to the back, feet, or shins. And, according to swimmers, it is more relaxing than jogging —you don't work up such a sweat and the water curling around your body can be soothing. In fact, swimming, or just sitting in swirling water, is the most common method of physical therapy for patients recovering the use of limbs, or learning to use them for the first time.

Bicycling:

You will have to invest in a bike, but it need not be an expensive one. It should, however, have at least 3 gears for a smoother ride. And if you plan to do most of your riding on streets and roads, buy yourself a protective helmet. One of the great advantages of bike riding is its practicality. If you live in a city you can ride your bike to work in about the same amount of time it would take on a subway or bus, and at the same time get your day's exercise. Or you can pack lunch and ride off with a friend on a day's outing without once thinking of exercise as a duty.

Other aerobic-oxygenating exercises are handball, and less effective, tennis and racquetball, because they are more intermittent and provide less over-all exercise than the others listed here.

Whatever exercise you choose, if you do it often enough and long enough, it will strengthen your heart so that it pumps more blood with every beat; it will increase the supply of red blood cells in your blood, thus increasing its oxygen-bearing capacity; it will develop brand-new circulation called collateral circulation—new capillaries actually grow as the result of exercise; it will increase the elasticity of your arteries, which need to constrict or expand depending on your body's particular demands; and it will, in combination with certain foods, clean plaque from the walls of your arteries. All this, in addition to what it will do for your emotional well-being!

And there are other needs—nourishment for the mind—that are fulfilled when we exercise in a regular and sustained way.

The need for movement: the need to run is always with us. As children, we run and move around when we play. As we grow, running becomes more institutionalized: we run for the ball in a football game or we run with others in a race. Once out of school, our style of living slowly squeezes the running out of us. But the need for movement never leaves us. We feel tired, worn out after sitting for eight hours in the office although we never actually exerted ourselves more than when we were playing a game of football at school. After a half-hour of exercise, we feel relaxed and mentally replenished.

The need for self-assertion: we spend much of our lives subjected to the rules of others—parents, teachers, bosses. We never have the chance to say: "This is me and you'd better take me as I am." Exercising is a socially acceptable way of asserting ourselves, of being as competitive with ourselves or with others as we want to be.

The need for both stress and relaxation: According to Dr. Hans Selye, each of us possesses at birth a given amount of "adaptational energy." When that energy is used up, we experience a mental or physical breakdown. One way to avoid such a breakdown is by deliberately creating stress in various parts of the body. A voluntary change of activity is often as good as or even better than rest. For instance, after a long hard day at the office, you might be so washed out that you dread the thought of running; yet as soon as you get started, you feel better, and by the end of a half-hour you are restored.

The need for mastery over ourselves: Mao Tse-tung wrote, in 1918: "In general, any form of exercise, if pursued continuously, will help to train us in perseverance."

Many of us are underdisciplined in our daily lives. By giving us something to struggle for and against, exercise provides an antidote to slackness. As Roger Bannister aptly puts it: "The urge to struggle lies latent in everyone and the more restricted our lives become in other ways, the more necessary it will be to find some outlet for this craving for freedom." Consciously or unconsciously, you are seeking the deep satisfaction, the sense of personal dignity, which comes when body and mind are fully coordinated and have achieved mastery over themselves.

The need to indulge ourselves: When we exercise regularly our physical condition is such that we can afford occasional excesses.

The need to forget ourselves, to submerge our egos: Sustained exercise is such an intense experience, both physically and psychologically, that we shed self-consciousness and live solely in the moment. Whenever we are involved in activities for their own sake, we become completely immersed in what we are doing and we lose our sense of self and time. We find, among other things, a vast increase in concentration.

The need to stop and think: Figuratively, that is what exercise time can mean. There is no intrusion from outside; we can think about specific problems, if we wish, or just let our thoughts wander. Many people have noted that after exercise something that has been bothering them will suddenly be solved, probably as a result of random, only half-conscious thought.

The need to make our own choices: During exercise our choices are entirely our own, not dependent on children or spouses or lovers. We can slow down, speed up, think or let our minds go blank, turn left or right, and what's more, make these choices spontaneously, without having to consult anything or anyone. We simply adjust our lives, during exercise time, to our own rhythms, our own strengths and weaknesses of the moment.

In short, exercise can make the difference. The options are mere existence or a full life. The choice is yours.

The exercise program that follows has been adapted in part from the President's Council on Physical Fitness. It will provide the kind of over-all conditioning needed for peak physical, mental, and emotional performance. Read it carefully before beginning.

How to Begin

If your physician has not selected an exercise program for you already, the tests described here will help you make the right choice. They will measure your present exercise tolerance and determine where you should begin in the walking-jogging part of the program.

Exercise capacity varies widely among individuals, even when they are similar in age and physical build. That's why your program should be based on your personal test results, rather than on what someone else is doing, or on what you think you should be able to do.

Walk Test:

The object of this test is to determine how many minutes (up to 10) you can walk at a brisk pace, without undue difficulty or discomfort, on a level surface.

- If you cannot walk for five minutes, you should begin with the RED walking program.
- If you can walk more than five minutes, but less than 10, you should begin with the third week of the RED walking program.
- If you can walk for the full 10 minutes, but are somewhat tired and sore as a result, you should start with WHITE walking-jogging program.
- If you can breeze through the full 10 minutes, you are ready for bigger things. Wait until the next day and take the Walk-Jog Test.

Walk-Jog Test:

In this test you alternately walk 50 steps (left foot strikes ground 25 times) and jog 50 steps for a total of 10 minutes.

Walk at the rate of 120 steps per minute (left foot strikes the ground at one-second intervals). Jog at the rate of 144 steps per minute (left foot strikes ground 18 times every 15 seconds).

- If you cannot complete the 10-minute test, begin at the third week of the WHITE program.

- If you can complete the 10-minute test, but are tired and winded as a result, start with the last week of the WHITE program before moving to the BLUE program.
- If you can perform the 10-minute test without difficulty, start with the BLUE program.

A Word of Caution:

If during these tests you experience nausea, trembling, extreme breathlessness, pounding in the head, or pain in the chest, stop immediately. If the symptoms persist beyond the point of temporary discomfort, check with your physician.

The symptoms described are signs that you have reached the limits of your present exercise tolerance. The point at which they occur will indicate where you should begin in the exercise program.

Your Exercise Program:

The routines described here employ the most up-to-date information available on exercise physiology. They are equally beneficial for men and women. Please follow instructions carefully.

The program consists of three parts:

1. EMM 1   Beginning
2. EMM 2   Intermediate
3. EMM 3   Advanced.

Each of the parts is divided (according to intensity) into three levels—RED, WHITE, and BLUE, with RED the least strenuous and BLUE the most difficult.

Warm-Up Exercises for Every Level

Standing Reach and Bend
  Starting Position:

Stand erect, feet shoulder-width apart, arms extended over head.
Action:
Stretch as high as possible, keeping heels on ground.
Hold for 15 to 30 counts.

Straight-Leg Back Stretch

Starting Position:
Stand erect, feet shoulder-width apart, arms at side.
Action:
Slowly bend over, touching the ground between the feet. Keep the knees straight. Hold for 15 to 30 counts. If you can't reach the ground at first, touch the top of your shoe line.
Repeat 2 to 3 times.

Alternate Knee Pull

Starting Position:
Lie on back, feet extended, hands at side.
Action:
Pull one leg to chest, grasp with both arms and hold for a five count. Repeat with opposite leg.
Repeat 7–10 times with each leg.

Double Knee Pull

Starting Position:
Lie on back, feet extended, hands at side.
Action:
Pull both legs to chest, lock arms around legs, pull buttocks slightly off ground. Hold for 20 to 40 counts.
Repeat 7–10 times.

Torso Twist

Starting Position:
Lie on back, knees bent, feet on the ground,* fingers laced behind neck.

* For best effect secure your feet under something to prevent them from lifting during action.

Action:

Curl torso to upright position and twist, touching the right knee with the opposite elbow.

Return to starting position.

Repeat, twisting the opposite direction. Exhale on the way up, inhale on the way down. Repeat 5–15 series.

Conditioning Exercise for Men and Women

The following exercises are for both men and women and provide basic over-all body conditioning.

Abdominal:

Select the one for you:

Head and Shoulder Curl (Beginner)

Starting Position:

Lie on back, legs straight, arms at sides.

Action:

Count 1—Curl head and shoulders off floor to a sitting position. Hold this position for 10 counts.

Count 2—Return to starting position.

Suggested repetitions: 10–15.

Situp, Arms Crossed (Intermediate)

Starting Position:

Lie on back, arms crossed on chest, hands grasping opposite shoulders.

Action:

Count 1—Curl up to sitting position.

Count 2—Curl down to starting position.

Suggested repetitions: 10–15.

Situp, Fingers Laced (Advanced)

Starting Position:

Lie on back, legs extended and feet spread one foot apart, fingers laced behind neck.

Action:

Count 1—Curl up to sitting position and touch right elbow to left knee.

Count 2—Curl down to sitting position.

Count 3—Curl up to sitting position and touch left elbow to right knee.

Count 4—Curl down to starting position.

Suggested repetitions: 15–25.

Shoulder—Arm:

Horizontal Arm Circles (Beginner)

Starting Position:

Stand erect, arms extended sideways at shoulder height, palms up.

Action:

Make small circles backward with hands and arms.

Reverse, turn palms down and do small circles forward.

Suggested repetitions: 15–20.

Giant Arm Circles (Intermediate)

Starting Position:

Stand erect, feet shoulder-width apart, arms at sides.

Action:

Bring arms upward and sideways, crossing overhead, completing a full arc in front of body.

Do equal number in each direction.

Suggested repetitions: 10.

Arms, Legs and Thighs:

When doing these exercises, it is important to keep the back straight. Start with the knee pushup and continue for several weeks until your stomach muscles are sufficiently toned to keep your back straight. Then try the intermediate.

Knee Pushup (Beginner)

Starting Position:

Lie prone, hands outside shoulders, fingers pointing forward, knees bent.

Action:

Count 1—Straighten arms, keeping back straight.
Count 2—Return to starting position.
Suggested repetitions: 5–10.

Pushup (Intermediate)
Starting Position:
Lie prone, hands outside shoulders, fingers pointing forward, feet on floor.
Action:
Count 1—Straighten arms, keeping back straight.
Count 2—Return to starting position.
Suggested repetitions: 10–20.

Quarter Knee Bends (Intermediate)
Starting Position:
Stand erect, hands on hips, feet comfortably spaced.
Action:
Count 1—Bend knees to 45 degree angle, keeping heels on floor.
Count 2—Return to starting position.
Suggested repetitions: 15–20.

Sitting Single Leg Raises (Advanced)
Starting Position:
Sit erect, hands on side of chair for balance.
Legs extended at an angle to floor.
Action:
Count 1—Raise left leg waist-high.
Count 2—Return to starting position.
Repeat equal number with opposite leg.
Suggested repetitions: 10–15.

Side Lying Leg Lift (Advanced)
Starting Position:
Lie on right side, leg extended.
Action:
Count 1—Raise left leg as high as possible.
Count 2—Lower to starting position.

Repeat on opposite side.
Suggested repetitions: 10–15.

Back Leg Swing (Advanced)
Starting Position:
Stand erect behind chair, feet together, hands on chair for support.
Action:
Count 1—Lift one leg back and up as far as possible.
Count 2—Return to starting position.
Repeat equal number of times with other leg.
Suggested repetitions: 20.

Heel Raises (Beginner)
Starting Position:
Stand erect, hands on hips, feet together.
Action:
Count 1—Raise body on toes.
Count 2—Return to starting position.
Suggested repetitions: 20.

Circulatory Activities

EMM 1—*Beginning*

RED: Walking Program

WEEK	DAILY ACTIVITY
1.	Walk at a brisk pace for 5 minutes, or for a shorter time if you become uncomfortably tired. Walk slowly or rest for 3 minutes. Again walk briskly for 5 minutes, or until you become uncomfortably tired.
2.	Same as Week 1, but increase pace as soon as you can walk 5 minutes without soreness or fatigue.
3.	Walk at a brisk pace for 8 minutes, or for a shorter time if you become uncomfortably tired. Walk slowly or rest for 3 minutes. Again walk briskly for 8 minutes, or until you become uncomfortably tired.

WEEK	DAILY ACTIVITY

4.   Same as Week 3, but increase pace as soon as you can walk 8 minutes without soreness or fatigue.

When you have completed Week 4 of the RED program, begin at Week 1 of the WHITE program.

EMM 2—Intermediate

WHITE: Walking-Jogging Program (Roving)

WEEK	DAILY ACTIVITY

1.   Walk at a brisk pace for 10 minutes, or for a shorter time if you become uncomfortably tired. Walk slowly or rest for 3 minutes. Again walk briskly for 10 minutes, or until you become uncomfortably tired.

2.   Walk at a brisk pace for 15 minutes, or for a shorter time if you become uncomfortably tired. Walk slowly for 3 minutes.

3.   Jog 20 seconds (50 yards). Walk 1 minute (100 yards). Repeat 12 times.

4.   Jog 20 seconds (50 yards). Walk 1 minute (100 yards). Repeat 12 times.

When you have completed Week 4 of the WHITE program begin at Week 1 of the BLUE program.

EMM 3—Advanced

BLUE: Roving Program

WEEK	DAILY ACTIVITY

1.   Jog 50 seconds (125 yards). Walk 1 minute (100 yards). Repeat 10 times.

2.   Jog 1 minute (150 yards). Walk 1 minute (100 yards). Repeat 8 times.

3.   Jog 2 minutes (300 yards). Walk 1 minute (100 yards). Repeat 6 times.

4.   Jog 4 minutes (600 yards). Walk 1 minute (100 yards). Repeat 4 times.

WEEK	DAILY ACTIVITY
5.	Jog 6 minutes (900 yards). Walk 1 minute (100 yards). Repeat 3 times.
6.	Jog 8 minutes (1200 yards). Walk 2 minutes (200 yards). Repeat 2 times.
7.	Jog 10 minutes (1500 yards). Walk 2 minutes (200 yards). Repeat 2 times.
8.	Jog 12 minutes (1700 yards). Walk 2 minutes (200 yards). Repeat 2 times.

Nutrition

Solar energy is the source of all life on earth. It reaches the edge of the earth's atmosphere at the rate of 2,000 million calories per second; of this, 30 percent is reflected and 20 percent absorbed by the atmosphere. Of the remaining 50 percent that reaches the earth's surface, at a rate of about 100 calories per square foot per day, 71 percent irradiates areas of water, 29 percent land. Since only about a third of the earth's land surface is part of the food chain as arable or pasture land, only about 3 percent of the sun's light actually irradiates green plants on the land or algae in the sea. The plants then convert about 1 percent of the energy reaching them into stored chemical energy via the process of photosynthesis.

When plants are consumed as food, about 10 percent of their stored energy is retained by the animal that eats them, and when that animal is eaten by other animals, about 10 percent of its stored energy is in turn retained by the eater.

All living things require energy to repair themselves, sustain activity and perpetuate the growth process.

Most plants get their energy from inorganic (nonliving)

materials. Chemicals drawn from the soil (water) and the air (carbon dioxide) are processed into food in the presence of sunlight. This simply means that plants are able to build complex food substances, carbohydrates, from some of the most simple and basic elements on earth.

On the other hand, animals use few natural inorganic materials, and can manufacture only a limited amount of food substances within their bodies. For them, food is the primary source of chemical energy. The chemicals required for their bodies' metabolic activities are broken down from the complex substances in food.

So plant synthesis of sunlight is the starting point for energy transference: energy and matter are passed on, thereafter, as one life form consumes another. Therefore you reach the energy sources synthesized by plant life—fruit, grain, vegetables—immediately if you eat the plants directly, rather than getting them second-hand by eating animals On the other hand, plant life is unable to provide some of the essential building blocks necessary for human protein.

Amino acids are the basic building blocks of life, and they are found in every life form on our planet, animal, or vegetable. Proteins, found in every part of the body—muscles, bones, eyes, hair—are made up of long strings of about twenty different kinds of amino acids. These few amino acids can combine to make billions of different kinds of proteins. In fact, 60 percent of the dry weight of the human body consists of protein.

Our cells manufacture proteins from simple amino acid building blocks, but the amino acids themselves cannot be manufactured, and must be obtained from our diet. However, cells have considerable capability to make some amino acids from others. Out of all the amino acids found in human protein, only eight cannot be constructed from any other amino acids; but these eight themselves can be converted into any one of the other seven amino acids. These eight essential amino acids are: Leucine, Isoleucine, Valine, Lysine, Methionine, Phenylalanine, Threonine, and Tryptophan.

In order for our cells to build a particular protein molecule, all of the essential amino acids needed for that molecule have to be available at the same time. If some of these amino acids were not in a meal then that protein cannot be built. Moreover, the job cannot wait till the next day in the hope that a new meal will bring in the missing amino acids, because by then the previous day's amino acids have either been used or excreted. They are not saved. It is thus vital that your meals should contain all of the eight essential amino acids. What that means, essentially, is a combination of unprocessed meat, vegetables, and grains of a sufficient caloric quantity to sustain life: this kind of diet will provide all of these essential substances.

Vitamins are organic chemicals found in food in extremely minute amounts. They are essential for the regulation of chemical processes within our bodies and therefore play a vital role in growth, development, and protection against illness and disease. The body cannot manufacture vitamins, so the presence of vitamins in food is crucial. Chemically, most vitamins are used by the body as part of its many enzymes. Enzymes are necessary to build particular parts of complex body chemicals. They are, within each cell, like men on a production line. The enzyme itself is a large protein molecule, coupled to one or two smaller molecules called co-enzymes. Most vitamins are co-enzymes. Since the enzyme cannot work without the support of its co-enzymes, any molecule that is being built by the enzyme therefore could not be completed without the particular co-enzymes required for that process. So when a particular vitamin is in low supply or absent from the body, the body cell machinery fails to function efficiently. The result is an illness specific to the role played by that particular vitamin. It should be noted, however, that not all vitamins are co-enzymes and not all co-enzymes are vitamins. Forty-one vitamins have been identified to date, and the usefulness of all of them in the human body has not yet been established.

Vitamins in the diet can be divided into two classes: those soluble in fat (vitamins A, D, E, and K) and those soluble in water (vitamin C and the B-complex vitamins).

The following vitamins have been found to be necessary to the human body, but scientists have not yet determined what their exact functions are or in what quantities they must be present.

Vitamin A
Vitamin C
Vitamin D
Vitamin E
Vitamin K
The B-complex vitamins:
Thiamine (B_1)
Riboflavin (B_2)
Niacin (B_3)
Vitamin B_6
Vitamin B_{12}
Folic Acid
Vitamin B_{13}
Vitamin B_{15}
Vitamin B_{17} (Laetrile)
Biotin
Choline
Inositol
Para-aminobenzoic acid (PABA)
Pantothenic acid

Minerals, like vitamins, do not supply any heat or energy to the body, but play a vital role in the regulation of body fluids and the balance of its chemicals. They are required by the body in varying amounts. Those needed in comparatively large quantities are called macronutrients, and they include calcium, phosphorus, sodium, chloride, potassium, sulphur, and magnesium. Micronutrients are those minerals which are required in smaller quantities, and they include iron, iodine, fluorine, zinc, selenium, manganese, copper, molybdenum, cobalt, and chromium. There are also trace elements which are found in the body in minute amounts but their functions have not been fully determined. They include strontium, bromine, vanadium, gold, silver, nickel, tin, aluminium, bismuth, arsenic, and boron.

The Chemical Value of Some Common Foods

1. Most meats are very rich in amino acids but are rather poor in supplying most of the major minerals, some of the trace minerals and certain vitamins, especially vitamins D and K.

2. Most cereals do provide an adequate supply of amino acids but they are very deficient in terms of minerals and most vitamins.

3. Beans, potatoes, corn, peas, and other similar foods seem to furnish a very well-balanced supply of most of the "growth and maintenance" chemicals except for chloride, sodium, chromium, vitamin B_{12}, and vitamin D.

4. Most vegetables also contain all the needed chemicals, except, again, for vitamins B_{12} and D and some of the minerals like chloride and sodium.

5. Fruits like oranges, apples, and watermelon are important for their chemical nutritional value but don't provide large amounts of amino acids.

6. Eggs and milk have an abundant supply of amino acids, and contain a majority of the vitamins but are insufficient in supplying most minerals.

In addition, we would also like to point out that sugar,

glucose, alcohol, starch, and saturated fat contain no maintenance chemicals at all.

Chemicals Essential to Your Emotional Health

Vitamin B Complex

All B vitamins are water-soluble substances which can be cultivated from bacteria, yeast, fungi, and molds. The known B-complex vitamins are B_1 (thiamine), B_2 (riboflavin), B_3 (niacin), B_6 (pyridoxine), B_{12} (cyanocobalamin), B_{13} (orotic acid), B_{15} (pangamic acid), B_{17} (laetrile), biotin, choline, folic acid, inositol, and PABA (para-aminobenzoic acid). The grouping of these compounds under one vitamin, B, seems to be mainly an accident of history, and in fact many of the B vitamins are now simply called by their chemical names. They do, however, tend to occur in the same foods, and perform many similar functions in the body. In fact the B vitamins are the single most important group of chemicals necessary for the proper functioning of the brain and the entire nervous system. They are also essential for the maintenance of muscle tone in the gastrointestinal tract, for the health of the skin, hair, eyes, mouth, and liver, and in the metabolism of fat and protein.

Their presence or absence in the body affects mood and the ability to concentrate and sleep, and can make us more or less tense and irritable. They are used in the treatment and cure of such nervous system diseases as multiple sclerosis, epilepsy, meningitis, Parkinson's disease, stroke, Bell's Palsy. They are of essential importance in the megavitamin cure for schizophrenia.

All the B vitamins except B_{17} are natural constituents of brewer's yeast, liver, or whole grain cereals. Of these, brewer's yeast is the richest natural source of the B-complex group. Other dietary sources include rice polishings, wheat germ, peanuts, bran, soybeans, peas, eggs, kidneys and other organ meats, oysters, pork, poultry, milk, greens, and beans.

Some of the B-complex vitamins are central to emotional well-being through the nervous system they supply and maintain.

Choline

Choline is one of the B-complex vitamins and functions with inositol, another one, as a basic component of lecithin. In the body, choline is synthesized by the interaction of B_{12} and folic acid with the amino acid methionine. Primarily, the function of choline seems to be the dissolution of fats and cholesterol in the body and it is used to treat atherosclerosis and hardening of the arteries. But the function of choline that is of importance to us here is related to its role in forming acetylcholine, one of the brain's neurotransmitters. The health of the myelin sheaths which surround and insulate the nerves is also maintained by choline.

The richest source of choline is lecithin. Other rich dietary sources include meat, fish, egg yolk, liver, cheese, brewer's yeast, and wheat germ.

Niacin

Niacin exists mainly in three synthetic forms: niacinamide, nicotinic acid, and nicotinamide. It is effective in improving circulation and lowering the cholesterol level in the blood and is vital in the maintenance of healthy skin and digestive system tissues.

However, its most important benefits seem to be related to the maintenance and proper functioning of the nervous system. It has proven effective in preventing migraine headache, epilepsy, schizophrenia, and other mental illness.

Pure niacin is present only in relatively small amounts

in most foods. However, lean meats, poultry, fish, and peanuts are rich daily sources of tryptophan, the amino acid that can be converted into niacin in the body. Other dietary supplements such as brewer's yeast, wheat germ, and desiccated liver are also rich in tryptophan and contain a small amount of niacin.

PABA

Para-aminobenzoic acid is considered a "vitamin within a vitamin," occurring in combination with folic acid. PABA stimulates the "good" intestinal flora to produce such needed vitamins as folic acid and vitamins K and B_1 (thiamine). However, its most important use is as a component of procaine, an effective local anesthetic with many other qualities which help alleviate depression, migraine and tension headaches, and other ailments of the brain and nervous system. PABA has been most recently used in Gerovital H3, a new drug under investigation, thought to possess antidepressive, rejuvenating, and antiaging qualities.

PABA is found mainly in liver, brewer's yeast, wheat germ, and molasses.

Vitamin C (Ascorbic Acid)

Vitamin C is considered the least stable of vitamins. Its potency is easily lost when exposed to light, heat, and air which activate the oxidative enzymes.

Under stressful conditions, when the body's general metabolism is heightened, the tissue requirements for ascorbic acid are also increased. Vitamin C is thus most essential in emotionally stressful situations. It too is used as part of the megavitamin treatment of mental disorder, especially schizophrenia.

Vitamin C is present in most fresh fruits and vegetables like citrus fruits, tomatoes, bananas, broccoli, and others. It is also present in liver and shellfish. Natural vitamin C dietary supplements are prepared from rose hips, acerola cherries, green peppers, berries, and other greens.

Magnesium

Magnesium is an essential mineral which accounts for about 0.05 percent of the body's total weight.

It is involved in many essential metabolic processes: it activates enzymes necessary for the metabolism of carbohydrates and amino acids, and also assists the regulation of the acid-alkaline balance in the body.

Medical research has indicated that magnesium is important in controlling the way in which electrical charges are utilized by the body to induce the flow of nutrients in and out of cells. It has been successfully used in treatment of such nervous ailments as Parkinson's disease, multiple sclerosis, and other neuromuscular disorders, nervousness, tantrums, sensitivity to noise, hand tremor, general depression, and mental illness. Since magnesium works to preserve the health of the nervous system, it has also been used in controlling convulsions in pregnant women and epileptic patients.

Magnesium is found chiefly in fresh green vegetables, where it is an essential element of chlorophyll. Other excellent sources include raw, unmilled wheat germ, soybeans, figs, corn, apples, nuts, and other oil-rich seeds. It also occurs in fish, eggs, poultry, beef, pork, milk, and milk products. Dolomite, a natural dietary supplement, is also rich in magnesium.

Potassium

Potassium constitutes about 5 percent of the total mineral content of the body. It is found mainly in the intracellular fluid. Together with sodium, it helps regulate the distribution of fluids on either side of the cell walls. It unites with phosphorus to send oxygen to the brain and also functions with calcium in the regulation of neuromuscular activity.

Potassium is also important in enzyme reactions and the synthesis of muscle protein from amino acids in the blood; it stimulates nerve impulses for muscle contraction.

Potassium has been used extensively in treating high blood pressure which is directly caused by excessive salt intake. Since it is essential for the transmission of nerve impulses to the brain, it has been effective in the treatment of headache-causing allergies, insomnia, and hypertension.

Large amounts of potassium are found in potatoes, especially in the peelings, and in bananas. It is also present in all vegetables, especially green leafy ones, oranges, whole grains, sunflower seeds, and mint leaves.

Where To Find These Vitamins and Minerals in Richest Supply

Brewer's Yeast

Brewer's yeast, which is available in powder, flake, and tabular form, is a nonleavening yeast. It is one of the best sources for the B vitamins and minerals. It contains 17 different vitamins, 16 amino acids and 14 types of minerals. The nutritional value of your diet is enormously enhanced with the addition of brewer's yeast.

The recommended supplemental amount is one tablespoon daily, which can be added to a glass of tomato juice, fruit juice, milk, or even sprinkled over salad or cereal. If you are trying to reduce, take it about 15 minutes before a meal because it will help take the edge off your appetite.

Wheat Germ

Wheat germ is the heart of the wheat seed and is sifted out during the manufacture of most flour. Many well-known nutritionists theorize that this wonder food may contain vitamins and minerals yet undiscovered, because animal experiments have shown that they receive various benefits not provided by known vitamins.

In addition, it has also been demonstrated that wheat germ can help lower the level of cholesterol in the body, improve energy levels, and even increase fertility and lessen complications of pregnancy and childbirth.

Wheat germ can be added to fruit drinks, cereal, casserole dishes, meatloaf and hamburgers. It can also be taken with fruits, as coating on fish and meat, on yogurt, and even as a handy substitute for some of the flour called for in baking.

Yogurt

Yogurt is milk fermented by a mixture of bacteria and yeast. The resulting custardlike product is then defatted and soured with Lactobacillus acidophilus and other digestive bacteria essential for the health of the intestine. It is high in protein content and vitamins A and D. It contains a higher percentage of the B-complex vitamins, especially B_6, than the milk from which it was derived. It is for this reason that it is included in the EMM diet.

Yogurt can be eaten either plain or seasoned with herbs or mixed with fruits. A word of caution: commercial yogurt may contain varying amounts of sugar or preservatives which tend to neutralize its therapeutic effects. Homemade yogurt is recommended.

Soybeans

Soybeans contain vitamins and minerals in a natural relationship that is similar to the human body's needs. In fact, a good supply of soybean products could serve as a major source of protein in a meatless diet. However, the proportion of essential amino acids supplied by soybean products is generally less than that of meats, so larger amount of soybean would be needed to supply those amino acids.

A variety of soybean products are available in the market. Soy flour, oil, and milk are some of the most common ones. Soy flour is a rich source of protein, vitamin B complex, iron, calcium, potassium, magnesium, and phosphorus. Soybean oil contains lecithin, a rich source of choline, and vitamin E which enables it to remain stable against oxidation and flavor deterioration. Soy milk is rich in iron, thiamine, and niacin but low in fat, carbohydrates, calcium, and phosphorus.

Other forms of soybean products are also sold as commercial imitation-meat items; pressed soybean cakes and sprouted soybeans even contain increased amounts of vitamin C.

Nuts

Nuts are the dry seeds or fruits of some types of trees or plants, with the edible meat or kernel enclosed by a hard covering or shell. They are a rich source of protein, unsaturated fats, B-complex vitamins, vitamin E, calcium, iron, magnesium, potassium, copper, and phosphorus.

Some of the common, most nutritious nuts are peanuts, sunflower seeds, cashews, almonds, walnuts, Brazil nuts, pecans, and filberts. They can either be eaten fresh, roasted, boiled, or in the form with flour or butter. Shells should be checked for firmness of the seal, since cracked nuts soon become dry and rancid. They should also be stored in airtight containers to preserve freshness and to prevent oxidation and rancidity of their fat content.

Fruits

Fresh fruits are good sources of vitamins and minerals, especially vitamins A and C. In fruits, carbohydrates are present in the form of cellulose and natural sugar; as such they are good substitutes for other high carbohydrate foods like candy, cookies and cakes which contain few nutrients.

Most of the nutrients in fruits are found in the skin: be sure to wash thoroughly prior to eating so that any possible chemical residue is removed. It is also preferable to eat ripe rather than unripe fruits because ripe fruits contain simple sugars which are easily assimilated by the digestive system.

Apples and bananas contain valuable bulk fiber in the form of indigestible cellulose which is essential for regular bowel movement, and they are also high in magnesium content. Bananas also contain large amounts of potassium, important to the nervous system's functioning.

Dried fruits and canned fruits are not as beneficial as fresh or frozen fruits because a lot of nutritional value is lost in the process of drying and canning.

A carbohydrate diet is essential for the manufacturing of serotonin.

Meats

Meat is ranked as the most important source of first-class protein. It is also a rich source of the B-complex vitamins (especially thiamine and riboflavin), phosphorus, iron, sulphur, potassium, and copper.

Variety, or organ, meats are usually richer in vitamins and minerals than muscle meats. Liver, tongue, kidneys, heart, brains, and sweetbreads (pancreas glands of calves or lambs) are variety meats. Of these, liver is considered the richest source of complete protein and the B vitamins, especially riboflavin, niacin, and B_{12}. It is also rich in vitamins A, C, and D, iron, phosphorus, and copper. Owing to its high iron and vitamin B_{12} content, liver provides strong resistance against iron-deficiency anemia and pernicious anemia.

Meat should be used within two or three days after purchase when it's at its peak of flavor and nutritive value; ground meat and variety meats should be cooked within 24 hours to prevent loss of valuable chemicals and spoilage. Juices obtained during cooking normally contain the meat's most valuable nutrients, and they should be served together with the meat.

For the Balance, Choose From These:

Fish of all kinds, including water-packed canned fish.
Poultry of all kinds.
Lean meats.
Hard cheese, pot cheese, farmer cheese, cottage cheese (low calorie) but keep to a minimum because their effect on neurotransmitters is still unknown.
Vegetables: broccoli, spinach, Brussels sprouts, parsley, zucchini. A good rule of thumb is to choose the darker vegetables in each class—spinach, carrots—because they contain more vitamins and minerals.
Brown or wild rice.
Whole grain cereals, breads, flours, such as 100 percent rye, stone-ground whole wheat, whole grain cornmeal, soy, whole grain buckwheat.
Any fluids without sugar (eight glasses a day) including water, skim milk, fresh juices.
Margarine and polyunsaturated fats.
Stimulants and depressants like tobacco, caffeine, and alcohol are best totally eliminated from your diet and your life.

Two days a week, adhere to a light protein diet, and one day a week a heavy carbohydrate diet—this means fruits and vegetables, *not* desserts and refined sugars! This rotation method gives the body a better chance to manufacture essential neurohormones and build an active serotonin reserve. One day a week is recommended as a fast day—fluids and fruit
    When planning your meals, try to keep the following juices only.

percentages in mind. Although you certainly can't measure these figures accurately, they represent an ideal dietary goal and meet all nutritional requirements:

12 percent protein
30 percent fats (divided equally between saturated animal fats and polyunsaturated vegetable fats)
48 percent carbohydrates from natural sources—complex carbohydrates
10 percent carbohydrates from refined or processed sugars

Our Diet and the Brain

According to Dr. Richard Wurtman of M.I.T., there may be as many as 50 different types of neurotransmitters, with about 30 identified so far. Dr. Wurtman also points out that the ability of brain neurons to make and release at least two of their own neurotransmitters—serotonin and acetylcholine—depends directly on the composition of the blood. Since the composition of the blood is directly dependent upon our diet, what we eat daily has a significant influence on the effective functioning of the brain.

Serotonin is formed from tryptophan, one of about 22 amino acids or building blocks of proteins which the body cannot manufacture by itself. The brain obtains this amino acid from the bloodstream, which in turn receives it from food intake. John Fernstrom, an associate professor of physiology at M.I.T., has demonstrated with his experiments on rats that meals of different kinds affect the amount of serotonin in the brain: high levels of protein lowers it and high levels of carbohydrates raises it. Other experiments with animals also show that large amounts of serotonin induce sleep and reduce appetite for more carbohydrates; low levels seem to be associated with the secretion of pituitary gland hormones and create insomnia and increased sexual activity in both male and female rats. In one experiment, low serotonin made rats less sensitive to pain.

While experiments are under way to explore the relationship between food and serotonin in humans, presumably, high-protein meals such as steak, fish, and eggs would tend to make one more alert, while high-carbohydrate foods like spaghetti and potatoes would tend to induce sleep. This could be explained by the fact that protein consists of only about 1 percent tryptophan compared to so many other amino acids supplied by fish or steak so that tryptophan becomes competitively outclassed and less of it can reach the brain. On the other hand, the carbohydrate diet stimulates release of insulin, which lowers amino acid levels in the bloodstream. Thus there is a relatively higher amount of tryptophan compared to other neural amino acids and the proportion of tryptophan getting to the brain is thereby enhanced.

Another neurotransmitter, acetylcholine, is released by all neurons whose axons leave the brain and spinal cord. However, its immediate precursor, choline, cannot be made by neurons and must be obtained from the blood, which receives a small amount of choline from the liver and the rest from lecithin.

As pointed out by Dr. Wurtman, an insufficient supply of acetylcholine could bring about a mental disorder that affects thousands of people. Known as tardive dyskinesia, it causes grimacing and uncontrollable movements of the lips, tongue, and head. In one study at M.I.T., oral doses of choline brought dramatic improvements in nine of twenty patients with tardive dyskinesia; eight others had some improvement while one became worse.

This marks a new scientific principle: virtually any brain disease caused by an insufficient amount of choline should be potentially treatable. Judging from initial experiments by Dr. John Davis, professor of psychiatry at the University of Chicago, manic depression may be one such treatable disease.

In fact, normal human memory apparently depends upon an adequate supply of acetylcholine. Thus meals rich in choline might prove helpful in boosting a failing memory; one large omelette can increase acetylcholine reserves within a few hours.

What we eat certainly influences what we are!

The EMM Diet

Now that you know some of the basics of good nutrition vis a vis your nervous system, and through it, your emotional well-being, you will understand the importance of following the EMM diet as part of your Lifelong Maintenance Program. The EMM Diet incorporates all of the recommendations implicit in diet research findings over the last fifteen or so years and it is not a faddist diet. It is a well-rounded program built on basic nutritional principles, and stresses the addition of a few foods that are high in the vitamins, minerals, and amino acids that are the foundation of a healthy nervous system.

Every Day:

1 tablespoon brewer's yeast.
¼ cup wheat germ.
Fruit—your choice.
1 banana or 1 baked potato *with skin*.
1 serving of a legume (peas, lima beans, lentils, soybeans) or
    spinach, broccoli, or lettuce.
2 servings of a vegetable or fruit with high vitamin C content.

Once or Twice a Week:

Lean meat.
Eggs as a main course.
Unsweetened bran cereal.

Homemade yogurt, or plain Bulgarian culture yogurt (Continental is the best known).

Nuts: unsalted and raw are preferable.

Foods that Are Good for You

Apples
Apple juice
Apple sauce
Apricots
Asparagus
Bananas
Barley (pearled)
Beans (white, red, pinto, calico, red Mexican, black, brown, Bayo, lima)
Bean sprouts
Beef (lean steak, roasts, hamburger)
Beets
Blackberries
Blueberries
Breads
Breakfast foods:
Bran
Broccoli
Brussels sprouts
Buckwheat flour
Cabbage (red or green)
Cantaloupe
Carrots
Cauliflower
Celery
Chard
Cheese:
 Cottage cheese (made
 from skim milk)
 Farmer's cheese
 Hoop cheese
Cherries
Chicken (without skin)
Chickpeas or garbanzos
Collards
Corn
Cornbread
Corn grits
Cornmeal
Cracked wheat
Crackers (no saltine)
Cranberries
Cream of Wheat (regular)
Cucumbers
Currants
Eggplant
Endive or escarole
Farina
Fish:
 Blue fish, cod, flounder, haddock, halibut, herring, mackerel, salmon, trout
Grapefruit
Grapes
Grape juice
Guavas
Honey
Honeydew melon

Kale
Kohlrabi
Lemons
Lemon Juice
Lettuce
Lentils
Limes
Macaroni
Mangos
Milk (skim, dried skim)
Mushrooms
Muskmelons
Mustard greens
Nabisco Shredded Wheat
Nectarines
Noodles (without eggs)
Oat cereal
Oatmeal or rolled oats
   or steel-cut oats
Okra
Onions
Oranges
Papayas
Parsley
Parsnips
Peaches
Peas
Peppers (green or red
   bell peppers)
Persimmons
Pimientos
Pineapple
Pineapple juice
Plums
Potatoes
Prunes

Prune juice
Pumpkin
Quaker Grits
Quaker Oats (old fashioned)
Radishes
Raisins
Raspberries
Rhubarb
Rice (brown, wild)
Roman Meal
Rutabagas
Rye wafers (unsalted)
Sauerkraut
Soup (without sugar, oil,
   or additives)
Soybeans
Spaghetti
Spinach
Squash (all varieties)
Strawberries
Sweet potatoes
Tangerines
Tomatoes
Tomato juice
Tortillas (corn)
Turkey
Turnips
Turnip greens
Veal (lean)
Vinegar
Watermelon
Wheat flours (whole,
   unbleached)
Wheat Hearts
Wheat Nuts
Yogurt

Foods You Should Avoid

Fats and oils: Fatty hamburgers, fatty steak, and the like.
Sugars: Refined sugar; pies, cakes, and pastries.
Breads, cereals, and other foods containing sugar.
Salt: Salty products such as crackers and salted herring.
Cholesterol: Animal organs, brains, liver, animal skin, shell-fish, eggs. Obviously some of these foods are good for you, but consume them in limited quantities only.
Coffee and tea.

The 8-Point Tune-up and Prescriptions for Maximum Performance

The 8-Point
Tune-up

You have gone through a unique life experience by making contact with your emotional self through the crash program. And by following the weekly regimen you can maintain and nurture that contact and, with small effort, keep your mind and body ready to meet unsettling emotions. But what about those important life situations? Those intersections that you are continuously taking and crossing? What are they most likely to be? What can you do when emergencies arise? How can you stay in perfect working order and tune yourself up for maximum performance? Here is a tune-up program that will help you realize your full potential, and polish your emotional vehicle.

Our staff of psychologists has determined that there are eight commonly recurring emotional areas in life. A brief description of each follows. Take a look at them now; think about them for a moment in relation to your own life. The balance of this section will deal with them in more detail, because we want you to have some background information on each, in order to help you recognize and be prepared for problems within each area. In that way, you will be able to detect warning signals in advance and diagnose them. And finally, you will learn to prescribe emotional cures for yourself.

1. *Identity*. Your identity is who you are—to yourself and to others. It is the sum total of a succession of selves that develops as you grow up within your family, and then among other important people in your life. Some aspects of identity will expand with reinforcement; others will atrophy when confronted with negative results. But your identity is always in a process of becoming.

2. *Change*. Dealing with sudden, drastic events is a tremendous task for your mind and body. They are required to perform, immediately and efficiently, in a new way. Even minor changes, even apparently pleasant alterations in the normal routine—vacations, outstanding personal achievement, and success—are possible problem areas for all of us.

3. *Growth*. To some degree, we all, in psychological parlance, wear masks, play roles. We act differently with different people, in different situations. In order to grow, to realize the unique individual within ourselves, we have to minimize this play acting and throw off the self-imposed chains of "what will everyone think if I don't live up to what I think are their expectations of me?" To grow, therefore, is an act that will demand your strength and courage.

4. *Relationships*. Our beings lie at the center of a network of relationships—lovers, husbands, wives, parents, children, friends, co-workers. These interconnections with others can be rewarding and mutually fulfilling, or they can be fraught with anger, frustration, guilt, hatred. Long-term close relationships must necessarily change, because the people who comprise them grow and change. And they can end, which means another sort of adjustment, and often loneliness, or at the other extreme, happy anticipation.

5. Conflict. There is no way to avoid conflict; every time we make a choice, no matter how minor, we are in a state of conflict. It is as useful as it is unavoidable; it makes us stretch, it sharpens us, it forces us to act in life's arena. But it can get out of control, wedging us into situations that damage our self-image, or render us incapable of action, creating anxiety, making us ill with hypertension and heart disease. By learning to identify the conflict, and making and adhering to decisions, we can minimize it.

6. Stress. Stress is the response of the body—physically or mentally—to any demand made on it. The demand can arise from a conflict situation or from your environment—for example, an annoying noise in the shop you work in. A stressful situation can last for seconds, or can become chronic. Like conflict, it is not inherently undesirable, but it must be controlled: if no demands for blood were made on our hearts by our organs, our hearts would stop!

7. Sleep. When we lack sleep we feel irritated, we can become irrational; we can, at further extremes, suffer from hallucinations, become mentally deranged, even insane. All of these symptoms are signals from the brain telling you that it can no longer control the body's functions without temporary rest. There are different types of insomnia, signaling different sorts of emotional disturbance. And there are new ways of curing it that are more in tune with the body's ecology than any of the array of barbiturates prescribed until recently.

8. Depression. Depression can be a result of change that brings loss, or it can be defined as learned helplessness in a stressful situation that has become chronic and seemingly insurmountable. Current research also indicates that depression can be caused by imbalances in our biochemistry. It is the most widespread of emotional ills, but, unfortunately, most of its victims do not recognize it in its chronic, most dangerous state, and they do nothing to help themselves, unaware that it is a treatable disease.

For each of the next eight days, we are going to ask you to read one of the following sections. This assignment is not to be considered a part of the four hours a week that you devote to your Lifelong Maintenance Program. It is a one-time-only assignment, to familiarize you with possible future trouble spots. As you complete each section, refer back to the 8-Point Tune-up Checklist on page 149, check off the date you completed reading each section, and make note of any observations, in the box provided or on a separate sheet of paper, that might help you whenever problems arise in any of these areas.

We do want to emphasize that you are expected to, and should, read over and administer prescriptions to yourself in any area that presents future difficulties. You *should* consider this maintenance work part of your Lifelong Maintenance Program.

EMM TUNE-UP CHART

	Date of Check Up	Notes
Identity RX		
Change RX		
Growth RX		
Relationships RX		
Conflict RX		
Stress RX		
Sleep RX		
Depression RX		

Identity

How you came to be the person you are, how your character evolved, is the product of a complex interaction of factors. Your identity continues to develop over your lifetime since the human organism is continually subjected to change by social agents. Although there are similarities between your early childhood and adult characteristics, there are also differences. Your family is an important factor in identity formation. The interests and attitudes of your parents strongly affect how you feel about yourself and how you relate to others.

Psychologists have identified three types of family structures, each of which places greater or lesser emphasis upon the importance of particular family members' needs.

1. A child-centered family is one in which the happiness and health of the children is the most important consideration. Parents willingly sacrifice their needs and desires for the sake of the children.

2. Home centered. In this type of environment, emphasis is given to the needs of the children but priority is placed on

maintaining personal relationships among all family members. Emotional security and companionship are highly valued.

3. Parent centered. Emphasis is placed on the needs and problems of the parents rather than the children. Most parent-centered families are committed to obtaining rewards and success from the community rather than the home.

RX *Prescription:* Family relationship.

Consider the family relationship you had as a child. How did it influence you. Identify the family member—mother, father, or caretaker, who was largely responsible for bringing you up—by checking the *four* characteristics that most accurately describe the person.

☐ 1. Secure	☐ 9. Sympathetic
☐ 2. Insecure	☐ 10. Empathetic
☐ 3. Realistic	☐ 11. Sharing
☐ 4. Unrealistic	☐ 12. Giving
☐ 5. Independent	☐ 13. Caring
☐ 6. Dependent	☐ 14. Outgoing
☐ 7. Communicative	☐ 15. Sensitive
☐ 8. Uncommunicative	☐ 16. Insensitive

Now repeat the test a second time, checking the four characteristics which most accurately describe *you*. Is there a resemblance? A similar pattern?

Regardless of family styles, an atmosphere of love and acceptance is important for the development of a healthy identity. All three of the styles mentioned are capable of providing family members with love and emotional warmth. Unfortunately, all three are also capable of producing an atmosphere of instability and hostility where love is not available to aid in identity formation and which may result in poor emotional growth for all family members.

It is well known that without love, the physical, mental,

and emotional development of children may be retarded. The warmth and affection of mothering and fathering are particularly important elements in the development of a healthy personality. The effects of its absence are evident in the personality characteristics of children raised in institutions and foster homes. Although these children's physical needs are adequately met, their strong emotional need for love and affection, normally supplied within the context of a family, remains neglected and unsatisfied. Without that satisfaction, children are much more likely to develop a poor sense of self and subsequently suffer emotional ills throughout life.

The family, important as it may be, is only one factor that contributes to the formation of identity. What we are is also based on what we expect of ourselves. Scientists have long known that a person's expectations for success or failure influences, to a large degree, his actual performance. Thus, if you feel that you will succeed you usually do. The "I don't think I can do this" syndrome usually leads to a self-fulfilling prophecy of failure. What we expect or believe about our abilities is based on past performance and the clues that other people in the world give us about ourselves.

In our society, most of us are expected by family and friends to attain professional or financial success. These expectations, which begin at an early age, tend to foster in us a strong need. Psychologists call it the need for achievement. Parenting techniques are especially important in determining the degree of each individual's need for achievement. Mothers of children with high achievement needs tend to expect and encourage independence and accomplishment. Such mothers also expect achievement at an earlier age than do mothers whose children have a low need for achievement.

Parental expectations which are of primary importance for young children, gradually become less important than the expectations of significant other people in an individual's life, most notably friends and teacher-mentors. The effect other people have on your behavior is probably best thought of in terms of rewards and punishments. Any action you perform which is followed by reward—money, materials, praise—is likely to be repeated. An action followed by punishment—disapproval, rejection, failure—is likely to be abandoned. In this way, the rewards and punishments provided by others influence the expectations you have for yourself—that is, your identity.

Through this very system of reward-punishment, you can change your expectations. The key is to change the kinds of rewards and punishments you receive from others by altering the behavior that elicits them. Change the old stagnant patterns of your life, replacing them with new behavior, and you can rewrite your own script. This process of change will alter both your own expectations and others' and gradually a new identity will begin to take shape, one that you can control from its inception.

These are some of the factors contributing to the manner in which we and others perceive ourselves. Erik Erikson, the well-known psychoanalyst, has described the process of identity formation in terms of eight stages through which we all pass, and this chart has become a classic in the field.

Another basis for identity formation is your genetic make-up. Each of us has 23 pairs of chromosomes which determine our unique qualities. Our differences derive from the infinite combinations of genetic structures that make up our physical, mental, emotional, and social qualities.

Since genetic structure does indeed form the basis for the type of person we become, it is reasonable to assume that some aspects of our psychological make-up will also be inherited. Researchers have found consistent individual differences in the way people behave from birth, and baby nurses in the maternity wards of hospitals bear this out with on-the-job observation. These differences in newborns cannot be learned; they are inborn.

In summary, the identity you construct for yourself is based on your experiences in the world, how others react to

Erikson's States of Psychosocial Development			
	Crisis	Age	Outcome
I	Trust vs. Mistrust	0–1	Hope
II	Autonomy vs. Doubt	2–3	Self-control
III	Initiative vs. Guilt	4–5	Direction and purpose
IV	Industry vs. Inferiority	6–11	Competence
V	Identity vs. Role Confusion	12–18	Devotion
VI	Intimacy vs. Isolation	Young adulthood	Love
VII	Generativity vs. Stag-nation	Middle age	Production and care
VIII	Integrity vs. Despair	Old age	Wisdom

you, and the basic tendencies you brought into the world with you. Your home, parents, and early experiences may have been particularly important in shaping your personality, but it is also clear that the experiences you have now can change your personality for better or worse. The choice you make today significantly influences the kind of person you will be tomorrow. Your identity can be a product of choice. You are free to choose the range of experiences you want for yourself based on your desire to grow as a person, or to lie dormant, ignoring the world around you.

RX Prescription: Friends, a mirror of who you are?

Your experiences shape your identity. Probably the most important influence upon your adult identity is the circle of friends that surround you. Consider the types of friendships you have. How many of these people have positive qualities you would like to share? How many have negative qualities that may outweigh the positive? Think carefully about the friends you have and the kind of person you want to be. Friendships are such an important part of your life that you cannot afford to be oblivious to the characteristics of those closest to you. Do your friends genuinely like you? Think about it. Are there some who would like you to fail? Do your friends support and reinforce those qualities in yourself that you value most?

Change

Traumatic change is like a stab wound—to our psyches, to our values. Dr. Thomas Holmes and Richard Rahe of the University of Washington created a point scale to measure degree and impact of change, and found that people with high scores had a greater probability of serious illness. The death of a spouse, or divorce—increasingly prevalent in our society—bring changes in life patterns that can create profound feelings of frustration, disorientation, deep depression, and withdrawal. We need a strong reserve of self-confidence to cope with drastic change. When the traumatic event has been the loss of a job or a mate, the accompanying loss of confidence can create severe stress. Many people indulge in irrational behavior, have affairs with unsuitable partners. Others withdraw into apathy, inactivity, periods of deep sadness.

RX Prescription: How can you cope with change and preserve your identity through a period of change?

Keep the rest of your life as intact as possible; don't make any big moves, or even minor ones, until you have fully adjusted to the major upheaval. Staying in the same environment, keeping the same job, the same house, the same school, the same friends, helps prevent the mental or physical illness that can be brought on by trying to adapt to severe emotional shock.

The impersonal hand of fate is bound to deal you some changes that will alter the pattern of your life; if you can accept them and learn to deal positively with their impact you can minimize the accompanying emotional trauma. And even the most shocking changes, so difficult to accept, can lead to a broadening of opportunities, a discovery of new talents, a completely new life that can be even better than the old one.

Change is challenge; accept it as an opportunity for personal growth and keep looking ahead. Looking back, miring in self-pity, yearning for the past, only intensifies the effect of any loss. Change should be a time for marshalling resources, for old-fashioned blessing-counting, for renewing joy in small and simple pleasures.

Growth

What do I want for myself?

What do I want to be?

The concern for who you are, your purpose in life, the ultimate meaning of your existence is a search for self. The search continues throughout your lifetime as you try to understand your own pattern of thinking, feeling, and acting. As you learn to anticipate your thoughts and reactions in different situations, you undergo a process of change and growth.

Growth is, first and foremost, a matter of having the courage to be; to present yourself to the world exactly as you are without fear of reproach. This is by no means an easy task. Sidney Jourard wrote that we tend to hide behind masks and conceal our feelings and identity:

> *A choice that confronts every one of us at every moment is this: Shall we permit our fellow men to know us as we are now, or shall we seek instead to remain an enigma, an uncertain quantity, wishing to*

158

*be seen as something we are not? This choice has
always been available to us, but throughout history we
have chosen to conceal our authentic being behind
various masks. . . . We conceal and camouflage our true
being before others to foster a sense of safety, to protect
ourselves against unwanted but expected criticism, hurt,
or rejection. This protection is purchased at a steep
price. When we are not truly known by the other people
in our lives, we are misunderstood. When we are not
known, even by family and friends, we join the all too
numerous "lonely crowd."*

Here is a list of reactive masks: how many do you wear?

1. Painful	9. Mediating
2. Authoritative	10. Peaceful
3. Honest	11. Hurt
4. Persuasive	12. Brave
5. Sympathetic	13. Confident
6. Angry	14. Loving
7. Tender	15. Caring
8. Judgmental	16. Ecstatic

Role playing is a device most of us use to avoid what
we think will be negative reactions from others. In actuality,
the reactions of others, positive or negative, help us to grow
psychologically. By denying ourselves access to these reactions,
we remove the fodder necessary for growth.

What kinds of roles do we hide behind? Often, the role
is determined by the situation. Your social role changes according to the demands of the people with whom you interact.
Think of yourself and the kind of person you are at work.
Are you the same kind of person with your family? At par-
ties? In the company of strangers?

Another kind of role may be termed the personal image:

it represents what you think you are. The personal image and the social role need not correspond to each other. What you think you are and the impression others form of you are most often quite different. And often your personal image—the feelings you have about yourself—does not correspond to reality. In fact, most of us judge ourselves harshly. We picture ourselves as much less attractive, intelligent, skillful, or creative than we really are. The feelings and expectations we hold for ourselves make up our self-esteem . . . our protection . . . our security.

Psychologists have attempted to measure self-esteem by comparing subjects' ideal feelings about themselves to their true feelings. If there is a large discrepancy between the way you picture yourself now and the way you would like to be, your self-esteem may be low.

Self-esteem is very similar to self-confidence. Both are determined by your experience of effectiveness and competence in the world. The opinion of others is probably the most important influence in determining your degree of self-esteem. And the more successful you appear to be before others, the more likely it is that you will receive positive reinforcement— praise and recognition. As the amount of positive reinforcement from others increases, your personal image will begin to merge with your ideal image.

Finally, somewhere beneath the roles we play, each of us has a real face. For some, role playing has almost completely buried the real face; for others, the real face still appears in the company of close friends, relatives, or trusted others. Uncovering this true self is the goal of those who have journeyed in search of identity. By pulling away the layers of pretense and pride, the naked self may be exposed, a self not rigid and set, but in a constant state of change—change that results from growth.

Roles, however, can be useful as tools for change. If one chooses to change aspects of his or her personality and plays a role in keeping with this new image, eventually the role will become an actual part of that individual's personality. In other words, if you act something out long enough, and believe it, it becomes true.

Roles are also necessary for our survival in certain situations. You may feel free to act silly, show anger, indulge in self-pity with close friends or family, but that would certainly not be appropriate behavior for an office, or at a social gathering with strangers. Thus, for many of us, roles merely represent various aspects of our personalities which can be disclosed or hidden away depending on the situation involved. The important thing here is to be aware of how you use roles. Using them to bury your "true" self, to escape from problems, is neither healthy nor useful to your development as an adult.

If you are truly secure, you have a firm sense of your own identity. You relate easily to other people, are optimistic, self-reliant, and adventurous. If you are insecure, you lack an overriding sense of personal identity. The ordinary events of living often threaten your security, and you may be preoccupied with preserving yourself. You probably feel isolated, unloved, and discontent. You may be pessimistic, easily discouraged, and afraid to seek out new friends, activities, and interests.

Few individuals are, however, totally secure or insecure; most of us fit somewhere between the two extremes. Often, the kind of security image we assume is influenced by the situation in which we find ourselves. You may appear very secure among close friends but frightened and intimidated in an unfamiliar group. Only by getting in touch with your real image, by gaining insight into the nature of your identity, can you hope to discard the unrealistic mask. No matter where your true self lies on the security-insecurity scale, you will be happier and more open to the process of growing and becoming when you reduce the number of roles you must play for others.

By reducing the roles you play, you become more visible to others. You no longer live up to what you think are their expectations. You become an individual. We seem to have a basic desire to merge with the crowd, not to stand out or be different. There is security in joining the crowd, but something is lost, too: the possibility to be truly yourself, to be entirely free.

RX *Prescription:* Getting your act together.

In order to grow psychologically, you must drop some of the roles you play to cover your real identity. Just who are you? To what extent do you hide your true emotions?

The following descriptions apply in some degree to all of us. Consider each alternative and decide how well it applies first to your real self—your personal image—and then to your social self. Be honest in your evaluation of the real self. On a scale of 1–5, with 1 being not at all like your real self and 5 being very much like your real self, rate each description and put the appropriate number in the box at the left.

In the boxes to the right of each description, rate their difference or similarity to your social self on the same 1–5 scale.

When you have completed the ratings, compare the two boxes on each side of the descriptions. You will find several boxes where the numbers do not match. On the far right side of the page write down the differences between the numbers in the two boxes for each description. For example, if the real self description receives a 4 and the social description a 1, you would put a 3 on the far right side of the page. Just look at the difference in the two numbers; don't worry about plus or minus. All the numbers on the far right will be positive.

Finally, add up the differences to get your discrepancy score. Look at the score chart to get an idea of how close your social self is to your real self.

REAL SELF		SOCIAL SELF
☐	1. Careless and impulsive	☐
☐	2. Depressed	☐
☐	3. Lonely	☐
☐	4. Generous	☐
☐	5. Friendly and sociable	☐
☐	6. Nervous and anxious	☐
☐	7. Experienced and knowledgeable	☐
☐	8. Embarrassed easily	☐
☐	9. Intelligent	☐
☐	10. Angry	☐
☐	11. Self-controlled	☐
☐	12. Cheerful	☐
☐	13. Selfish	☐
☐	14. Shy	☐
☐	15. Cool and calm	☐

0–10   You are pretty honest in social situations. You seldom indulge in role playing. You are open for growth.

11–20   Your mask-wearing moments are infrequent. You are pretty honest about yourself.

21–30   You sometimes hide behind a role but this does not indicate you cannot grow.

31–40   You are afraid to open yourself in some situations.

41–50   You need to work on being more open. Try to reveal your real self.

A few years ago, a group of psychologists at a large university made up a personality profile that included the following:

You have a strong need for other people to like you and for them to admire you. You have a tendency to be critical of yourself. . . . Discipline and controlled on the outside, you tend to be worrisome and insecure

*inside. At times you have serious doubts as to whether
you have made the right decision or done the right
thing. . . . You have found it unwise to be too frank
in revealing yourself to others. At times you are extro-
verted, affable, sociable, while at other times you are
introverted, wary, and reserved. Some of your aspirations tend to be pretty unrealistic.*

The same profile was presented individually to a number of
college students who were told that a computer had determined their personality profiles based on available information
in school files. Amazingly, over 90 percent of the students indicated that this was a "good" or "excellent" interpretation
of their own individual personalities. Some commented that
the description was "true without a doubt" or "unbelievably
close to the truth."

This example points up the fact that most of us perceive
ourselves very similarly. We all feel, at times, insecure, worried,
and self-critical. The kinds of fears we have need not be har-
nessed, hidden from others, distorted, and denied. By accepting
the fact that your hopes and aspirations, your disappointments
and dissatisfactions, are no different from those of the vast
majority of others, you have taken a big step in realizing your
potential for psychological growth.

Emotional health is a relative term. It has been defined
in terms of conformity to social expectations, feelings of well-
being, the ability to function as a warm and open human being. Only recently have psychologists begun to associate psychological health with the ability to express your true self, to
get in touch with your identity and to expose it to others.

The initial step in the growth process is to realize that
your feelings, abilities, and interests are not that different from
other people's. It is okay to express yourself the way you are.

A second step in achieving emotional growth is the experience of competence. When you attain a desired objective
you feel competent. When the power of your body and your

mind is effectively used to solve a problem or reach a goal you feel competent. The experience of competence is the experience of success.

Competence develops selectively; each individual has different areas in which he or she feels more or less competent. I may feel very competent behind my desk at the office but not at all competent on the tennis court. Some individuals develop artistic or intellectual competence, others develop physical competence, and others develop social competence. Feelings of competence grow as skills develop, particularly when those skills are highly valued by other people.

If a person's attempts repeatedly end in failure, the result will be feelings of inferiority rather than competence. Such feelings can only heighten an individual's image of himself as valueless and lead him to constantly make unfavorable comparisons between himself and others. It is important to balance unsuccessful attempts to develop competence with a number of successes in areas in which you already feel competent. Fortunately, most of us feel fairly competent a great deal of the time because we tend to focus on activities in which we have special skills and experience. By validating our competence in these familiar areas, we build up enough self-confidence to explore new areas which we have previously avoided. In this manner, we are able to expand the boundaries of our competence without feeling inferior.

So, you may say, I do feel competent in some areas. I know that my needs and expectations are not so different from those of others. I feel very good about myself at times, but how do I become the kind of person I would really like to be? How do I gather up enough courage to remove the masks I wear, to open myself for growth? Am I really able to change myself, to become a more self-actualized person?

The answer is an emphatic yes. Personality and behavior are learned, flexible, modifiable; they hold the potential for growth. Your decision to change is itself a move toward growth; your intention is an important ingredient for growth.

RX Prescription

Look at growth as a sequence of levels. It is possible to work upward from one's current level to a higher, fully self-actualized level.

The following levels of psychological growth suggested by Dr. Morris Holland of UCLA have been constructed so that you may determine how you stand in relation to growth potential. The levels are numbered 1 to 4, with the fourth level representing the self-actualized, fully functioning person. Not many of us have achieved this level of growth, although you may recognize aspects of yourself there. The same is true of the other levels; you will recognize some aspects of yourself at each one. Try to appraise your overall personality and see which level best describes you. Levels you have not reached can serve as goals for your future development.

☐   LEVEL ONE
You are willing to talk about yourself; you talk only about externals—facts, not feelings. You don't recognize your own feelings; you lack congruence. You see yourself as static, constant, unchanging. You find close personal relationships with others dangerous and threatening. You maintain personal distance and tend to see others as objects. You live by external rules, values, and expectations; you are a conformist. You don't believe you have any problems.

☐   LEVEL TWO
You talk about yourself, but you see your true self as an object, separate from you. You are able to talk about personally meaningful feelings and experiences in the past or future, but you cannot communicate how you are feeling right now. You recognize your feelings but you don't accept them; you tend to see them as shameful or abnormal. You begin, with great self-consciousness, to risk relationships with others. You begin to search for your own internal rules and values, but you

still basically conform; you don't trust yourself yet. You recognize that you have problems, but you don't feel responsible for them.

☐ LEVEL THREE

You can communicate your feelings and experiences in the present; your feelings seem to "bubble up" in spite of your remaining fears and distrusts. Although you can express emotional experiences, you are often surprised and frightened by them, rather than pleased. You begin to have lengthy periods of selfless absorption, of unself-consciousness. You experiment with being nonconforming. You feel greater effectiveness in handling problems and making choices. You recognize the central importance of close personal relationships and can identify the problems you have in this area. You accept greater responsibility for your own problems.

☐ LEVEL FOUR

You can communicate your feelings and experiences freely, both verbally and nonverbally, as they occur. You are very aware of your own feelings; you accept them as being you. You trust your own impulses. You live very much in the present, experiencing what is, not trying to interpret and explain the present in terms of the past. You see yourself as changing, growing. Close, open relationships with other persons are highly valued. You can be nonconforming even at the risk of being unpopular. You can have strong feelings of competence and well-being and participate fully in the richness of life.

One of these four levels probably describes your general orientation toward life. Whether it is level one, two, three, or four, you have growth potential. Even those few people who reach the fourth level are still growing, still striving to reach their fullest potential.

Relationships

Relationships are such an integral part of our lives that we often take for granted the effort and involvement necessary to form meaningful connections with others. Because so much emphasis today is on doing our own thing, self-realization, self-expression, we may tend to neglect the relationships that form the foundation and framework of our lives. Healthy relationships sustain and support us, bring us much of the happiness we know.

What are the components of a good relationship? What distinguishes a healthy, fulfilling relationship from a crippling, self-effacing, emotionally draining experience? Most psychologists agree that a good relationship is based on mutual trust and communication.

Communication is a learned ability. As infants we rely on nonverbal forms of expression—eye movements, laughter, tears. As we mature intellectually, we learn to express our likes and dislikes verbally. However, the ability to use words does not necessarily result in communication. Total communication is the uninhibited expression of feeling and the commitment to understand another person. Total communication is a primary objective of relationships.

Trust is the second primary component. Feelings of trust depend heavily on the disintegration of the social roles we described earlier. Role playing protects our private world from external invasion. When we learn to trust another person, we allow that person to become a part of us; to join us in our flights and fantasies. The building of a strong relationship through mutual trust is one of the most rewarding and invigorating experiences we can have as human beings.

Relationships, however, can bring emotional pain, frustration, and sorrow. How does one instigate and promulgate significant relationships while at the same time avoiding the petty arguments, the headaches, the hassles of meaningless relationships?

We all have within us an incredible mechanism we can call a biocomputer. Within five minutes of meeting someone new, we can and usually do make some observations about that person. We might think, "This person could be my future lover, friend, pal, enemy, business associate, husband." The choice your biocomputer makes, based on your experience and instinct, is usually right. Learn to listen to yourself, to trust your instincts. If they're rusty with disuse, you might make some initial mistakes, but don't let that discourage you. If you use it often enough, your biocomputer will give you accurate and trustworthy assessments about people, and provide you with an early indication of the kind of relationship you might be able to enjoy.

The next set of questions is more difficult: what kinds of relationships are worthwhile, how do you maintain a relationship, and how do you cope with the void created by a broken relationship?

In the desperate search for new experiences, new sensations, more and more people are experiencing heartbreak, loneliness, and depression because they lack the ability to form and maintain close, sustaining relationships. They cling to the feeble security of the shallow relationships they already have and when these inevitably crumble, their own lives crumble with them. By choosing our relationships carefully and working at them, we can avoid these experiences and lead fuller and more productive lives in the company of others. The quality, not the quantity, of human relationships is the key to happiness.

A good relationship requires an open line of communication. This is more than the passing interaction that characterizes many of our exchanges with others. For those, most of us have at hand a ready supply of expressions for greeting, acknowledging, and parting.

The daily ritual sometimes demands no caring: words without meaning, touching without feeling, information exchanged without emotions, only mild recognition of the presence of one another. We use similar forms of interaction with various people in our lives. With some, perhaps those we haven't much investment in, we play a polite conversational game that involves hiding or falsifying our true feelings or intentions. With others, we speak from behind a veil of authority rather than on a person-to-person level.

By falling into patterns of emotional isolation, it sometimes becomes difficult to communicate effectively with the really significant people in our lives. The type of communication that builds and strengthens relationships involves an honest exchange of feelings and information. It is not ritualistic, not rehearsed. To truly communicate, you must be open with your thoughts and feelings; you must reveal yourself to others. There are inherent risks; such openness gives others the power to hurt you, but it also makes it possible for them to know you and like you. Without taking this risk in communicating, you have little chance for developing fulfilling relationships. Professor D. W. Johnson expresses it as follows:

There is much evidence that indicates that healthy relationships are based on self-disclosure. If you hide how

you are reacting to the other person, your concealment
can sicken the relationship. . . . Being silent is not being
strong; strength is the willingness to take risks in the
relationship, to disclose yourself with the intention of
building a better relationship.

RX *Prescription:* Conveying something important.

Most people don't read important documents, nor do
they listen to information of importance that concerns them.
If you want to make an important point, don't use more than
the first two minutes of conversation, or in the first ten lines
of written material in formulating your idea. You run the
risk of losing your audience after that; they will bring in their
own sequential ideas and judgments, building on what you
are saying, so that your original thought tends to get lost.
Everything you say or write after that initial period should
simply support your original idea. Abstract your conversa-
tions, talk about only what is new and relevant.

The Good and the Bad of Relationships

We sometimes find ourselves wondering just why we are
involved in certain relationships. Some are lacking in substance
and may even be destructive to us. Does the relationship exist
solely for mutual security? Or because neither party has the
courage to try to change or improve it?

Many of us seem to have an almost masochistic need for
someone who will put us down, give us the punishment we
may subconsciously feel we deserve. Like cleaning out a closet
and discarding clothes that no longer suit us, we should try to
rid our lives of negative relationships, prune away those that
are sapping us emotionally. In the brief time we have it is
important to find and build relationships that are mutually
supportive, where strength and understanding can be exchanged. We must stop looking for people who can do some-

thing for us, people we believe will validate us, give significance to our lives because of their accomplishments, their physical attributes, their importance in the world. Rather we should seek understanding, true compatibility, a sharing of pleasures large and small, friends to whom we can reveal our deepest, most hidden selves.

We are always changing, our relationships are changing; we must discard the ones that are harmful, strengthen and develop the positive ones, be open always to new possibilities of friendship, make even our most casual relationships brief encounters of brightness and joy.

Think about the different interpersonal relationships in which you are involved. What qualities do these relationships share? Good interpersonal relationships have special characteristics.

RX Prescription: Relationship review.

Doctors and the Psychology Department at UCLA developed the following questions to assess the qualities of your relationships.

☐ *Is it honest?*

Each of you can risk being honest with the other. You are not afraid to tell the other person what you are thinking and how you feel.

☐ *Is it supportive?*

You are mutually supportive and accepting of the other. You express your approval, praise, and appreciation of the other. You accept and value the other person just the way he or she is.

☐ *Is it deep?*

The relationship is between two "real" selves, not between the social or public impressions you try to create. Each of you feel you really know and understand the other in a personal, nonsuperficial way.

☐   *Is it meaningful?*

The relationship is a significant part of your life. What happens to the other and how he or she feels are matters of concern for you.

☐   *Is it transcendent?*

Each of you is involved with the life of the other in an unselfish way. You are not self-centered or egocentric in the relationship; you are not in it for what you can get out of it. The relationship transcends, or goes beyond, your selfish needs.

Emotional Stumbling Blocks:

In trying to establish ideal relationships, think about these stumbling blocks. These characteristics, on either your part or anothers, will interfere with the development of a good relationship.

☐   *Egocentricity*

A concern with one's own interests to the extent of being insensitive to the welfare and rights of others.

☐   *Deceitfulness*

A tendency, often accompanying egocentricity, to take an exploitative approach to interpersonal relationships. Sometimes deceit extends to outright lying and stealing, but more commonly it shows itself in the efforts of an "operator" to manipulate people and situations to his or her own advantage.

☐   *Overdependency*

A tendency to lean excessively upon others for either material aid or emotional support and to rely upon them for making decisions.

☐ *Hostility*

A tendency to be antagonistic and suspicious toward other people.

☐ *Inferior feelings*

A basic lack of self-confidence or self-esteem which may be expressed either in oversensitivity to "threat" or in exaggerated efforts to prove one's own adequacy and worth by such techniques as boasting, showing off, and being hypercritical of other people.

☐ *Emotional insulation*

An inability to make the necessary emotional investment in a relationship, for fear of being hurt.

The Dramatic Triangle

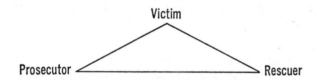

This sort of destructive relationship occurs in the following way: someone needs help or support; you step in as rescuer and get actively involved, the future payoff being self-gratification as a result of having "saved" someone. Instead, that someone turns on you because you have left him nothing with which to help himself: unless you know how to rescue, a drowning person will pull you down. Now you are the Victim. That angers you, because you were only trying to help. That anger makes you the Prosecutor; you now rail against the person you had previously tried to help.

RX Prescription: How to help.

If this mode looks familiar to you, follow these rules when someone reaches out to you for help:

1. Be a caretaker, not a rescuer. Show care and offer insight only.
2. Look out for your own sense of self; don't lose *yourself* in your attempt to help.

Improving Relationships

Strong, secure relationships are a vital part of your psychological well-being. One important component of your program for change should be the strengthening of relationships or the seeking out of new ones. Begin with your wife, husband, lover, friend—the major relationship of your life. If it's bad, get to work on it. If it's good, make it better. Usually what's needed is communication. Whether you have been married for twenty years, have just met what might be the love of your life, or are partway into a close relationship, the best way to evaluate and preserve it is through a regular program of written communication.

Many counselors recommend the written communication approach—an international marriage renewal program has used it successfully with 600,000 people. All you need are two notebooks and the courage to be frank; to let your partner see into your head and heart; to respond honestly and fully to the things revealed to you. In a budding relationship, it's a good idea to exchange lists of the things you like and don't like about the other person. Don't nit-pick or complain, just be totally open. Better to say some of these things now than to let them fester for the next ten years. And writing is much better than talking; few of us are really good listeners. We're always jumping in before the other person has really made his point, waiting for openings, saying things like "yes, but," "what if," and "if only," without hearing or responding to the point at hand. Write it out, exchange notebooks and you will be able to have a dialogue without interruptions and escalating tempers.

If yours is a long-standing intimate relationship it may be time to get those old smoldering grudges out in the open; at the same time let your partner know the positive things you feel. In the beginning you should exchange weekly lists, always stressing the positive as well as being completely frank about the negative. No name-calling, no jabs below the belt, no karate chops. This is not revenge but communication. Each week it will get easier and better; you will learn to appreciate each other more and find deeper understanding. Learning what your partner values in you as well as what drives him or her into a state of distraction is vital—you can then work on strengthening the one and reducing the other. You must work not only at being completely open and honest in your evaluation but at striving hard to understand exactly what the other person is trying to tell you. It might be wise to rephrase any sticky or sensitive points in your own words, to give feedback so that there is no possibility of misunderstanding.

In addition to working at communication, how do you improve relationships? If you give about 75 percent more than you would expect to receive, if you keep your sense of humor and take yourself and problems lightly, you're halfway home. Discuss your observations, explain your emotions, but don't criticize for the fun of it. Learn to understand the context of what your partner is saying. Be aware of the timing; strive always for perfect clarity, open listening, and feedback.

RX Prescription: How to register complaints and criticism constructively.

1. Don't draw comparisons between the person's behavior and someone else's.

2. Avoid sarcasm.

3. Don't repeat: make your point only once.

4. Don't obect to qualities or actions the person cannot control.

5. Don't apologize for your complaint.

6. Add something positive; give the other person something to go on with.

Coping with Endings

In spite of careful nurturing, relationships end, but endings as well as beginnings are an integral part of life. When relationships end people often become confused, frightened, guilty. The immediate goal is to get rid of the pain; a first step is acceptance. Epictetus said "True instruction is this: to learn to wish that each thing should come to pass as it does." If we cannot let go of a relationship, if we still keep clutching frantically at what no longer is, we do not make room in our lives for something new. In order to grow, to expand and improve our lives, we must develop the courage to turn away from a relationship that is no longer vital or healthy.

To move from intimacy, the life of "we" and "us," to living and making decisions alone, now only an "I" and "me," can be and usually is cataclysmic. But the careful nurturing of an inner life, of self-worth, of a calm strength that doesn't depend on the validation of others, is vital in easing the pain and moving forward. This is why we must make those emotional deposits and build reserves to carry us through those painful and difficult separations and endings. The strength that comes with personal growth is the essential component in the process of adapting effectively to the drastic life changes associated with the ending of relationships.

RX *Prescription*: Strokes.

Every day find one thing that you like about yourself and think about this several times during the day. You may like the way you look, or a thought or quality that you have, or a talent you are capable of. Write it down on your prescription pad.

Three times a day, "care" about three different people that you come into contact with; that is, look for something good about them. Compliment them, generate a pleasant feeling; this will add up to about 1,500 strokes a year. Other people will start feeling better about you, and you will start feeling better about yourself. By generating good feelings, you radiate and attract good feelings. You are like a mirror.

RX Prescription: A monthly "marriage" contract.

Every month write the following five points on a piece of paper, leaving room between them to fill in:

1. What I like about myself:
2. What I dislike about myself:
3. What I like about my partner:
4. What I dislike about my partner:
5. What I like about our relationship:

Your partner—your mate, lover, anyone with whom you have an intimate relationship—should do the same. Exchange lists, and after reading them, discuss modifications. When you talk, be sure to:

1. Discuss one point at a time.
2. Be patient.
3. Respond fairly.
4. Stay on the subject.
5. Don't switch the blame.
6. Try to reach a solution.
7. Be receptive.
8. Think of the other person and throw away your own pride and anger.

9. Set yourself a time limit of about an hour. Come to mutually satisfactory conclusions and write them down. In this way, you can have discussions, not arguments, with those people who are close to you.

Loneliness

Loneliness is a growing, spreading phenomenon in our cities; crowded with people, yet so many isolated, each in a separate box, connecting only briefly in their daily patterns. Tall apartments, clusters of condominiums, balconies filled with bright geraniums: behind them loneliness, an epidemic among the middle-aged, the old; an increasing problem in young adults. Look at me, speak to me, love me, need me— we fight it with television, singles bars, drugs, frenetic activity. We keep busy, but we aren't paying the slightest bit of attention to other human beings or even to ourselves.

During infancy we are totally and wholly cared for and nothing is expected from us in return; we try to recapture that blissful state for the rest of our lives. Solitude and aloneness are necessary for recharging the mind and soul and inspiring creativity. Loneliness, however, is a feeling of inward emptiness, of being unloved, unwanted, unfulfilled. What so many of us are really looking for is someone who will accept us, with all our real or imagined faults, who will give to us and care about us, demanding nothing in return.

We need to be aware of ourselves, but not so self-absorbed that we're unaware of or unconcerned about the world around us. Those concerned only with themselves generally live lives of loneliness, depression, and anxiety. In extreme cases they withdraw completely, wallowing in self-pity.

Too many of us were brought up believing we were unacceptable, not worthwhile. As a result we are deeply afraid of getting to know who we really are. Most of us were pushed to achieve, often by open comparison; someone pointing out to us how well our peers were doing. Unfortunately, it was an effective way to make us feel both insecure and inadequate. So we grow up afraid of involvement, afraid of failing and getting hurt.

Can we really expect to go through life without getting hurt? The real problem is that the child in us fears we won't get back all we give. That's what jealousy is all about; it is not proof of love, it merely indicates we are worried about our investment.

We all need the closeness and the rich human comfort and warmth that comes in a good marriage, within the bonds of long-time friendship, or in strong family associations. The importance of these bonds are often neglected and weakened in an era that puts so much emphasis on self: self-fulfillment, self-expression, self-sufficiency. And a lack of these essential human connections creates loneliness.

How can you escape loneliness? By recognizing that it is your job, and your job only, to weave connections with other people. No one is going to do it for you.

RX Prescription: Bursting the bubble around you.

Though it might sound paradoxical, the lonely person, withdrawn and self-absorbed, has to care *more* about himself because no one else does. To avoid loneliness you must become more self-accepting so that you can become more accepting of others. The lonely person, inadequate and insecure, is concerned about not getting what he needs from the world, but he doesn't do anything about it. Caring for yourself also means being a fairly firm disciplinarian, saying "no" to that extra drink, that extra amount of food; getting enough sleep and enough exercise; promoting your goals and ambitions. Then you will find it much easier to turn it around and apply that same care to other people. And that focus on the happiness and welfare of others will, provided it is given freely without thought of "repayment," release you from the prison of yourself. You must accept responsibility for your own behavior.

RX Prescription: Feeling good.

You are the only one responsible for your feelings, and you have the option to feel good or bad. If someone hurts you, you can choose to what degree you will let it affect you. This will not be easy at first, because we all grew up believing that other people had the power to determine our feelings. Get back that power, and don't ever give it away again!

RX Prescription: On boredom.

You can't eliminate someone else's boredom by trying to entertain them. You are not an entertainer. But that someone might find you boring because you yourself are bored. In that case you're the only one who can act. Reawaken your sense of curiosity and wonderment. Become actively involved with the people and activities in your life.

Conflict

We usually protect ourselves from anxiety through unconscious protective devices called defense mechanisms. The use of defense mechanisms is not abnormal; only when they come to dominate our lives and distort perceptions do they become dangerous.

Participation in life means constant conflict: the doctor facing surgery, the lawyer preparing a brief, the composer choosing the right note, the writer searching for the proper word, the student learning and understanding the appropriate material. We go through an average of 400 conflicts a day: what clothes to wear, what priorities and options to choose, where and in whom to invest our energy, how to spend each moment, each day.

RX Prescription

When we are acutely anxious our biochemistry changes; we become tense and our bodies undergo stress reactions. Recall the last time you felt anxious. What were you thinking?

What were your physical symptoms and what did you do about them? These are some common reactions to anxiety. How often have you used one of these mechanisms?

1. Repression—selective forgetting: "I can't ever remember doing that."
2. Reaction formation—When you were actually afraid and said "I am not afraid of anything."
3. Projection—"No one likes me." There is something wrong with you.
4. Rationalization—"I didn't get the job because of my ethnic background."
5. Displacement—Changing focus: "Well, remember the time *you* did that."

The skill of conflict resolution seems to have been built into our systems. For the most part, we make our daily decisions and carry on with our lives without undue anxiety about our choices. Conflict is taken care of unconsciously; only when the pending decision is extremely difficult or important does conflict rise to the surface of consciousness.

Unhappiness, worry, and frustration accompany difficult conflict situations where you are being pulled in different directions. You might not even be fully aware of the conflicting forces. The first step in gaining control of these forces and relieving the tension and anxiety that accompany them is to do just that.

Awareness implies understanding what the conflicts are, the sources of the conflict and what alternatives are available to you. We all have many different needs and desires. Sometimes a particular need may be incompatible with a need someone else has. This results in a social conflict. At other times one of your needs may compete with another of your needs; if both cannot be satisfied simultaneously, you are in a state of internal conflict.

Social conflict affects our lives in a number of ways. Since we live in society, it is inevitable that at times our needs and the group's needs are opposed. Some people try to avoid inevitable social conflict by becoming social isolates. Obviously, such a strategy doesn't work in the long run; it impedes our growth and development as human beings.

Social conflict is present in life from its very beginning. Our parents have certain expectations for us which may or may not have agreed with the expectations we ourselves held. Conflicts often arise from relationships between the sexes. We all have had the experience of feeling that we loved someone who did not love us. Our desires and needs involved the other person, because without the participation of the other, those needs could not be satisfied. But if that other person did not love us, a frustrating conflict resulted.

Conflict may also take place on a much broader scale. Each society or culture sets up certain expectations for its members—rules, laws, customs, and values. Those who do not. live up to these expectations are thought of as criminal, immoral, even insane. It is important to remember, however, that each member of a society is an individual and the individual's values differ in varying degrees from those of society. The greater the discrepancy between an individual's values and those of society, the greater the potential for conflict.

Societal expectations do change with time. For example, our own society's sexual mores have changed rapidly over the last 20 years. Many of us have suffered intense personal conflict as a result of failure to adjust to new value systems. One of the most important determinants of mental health is the ability to adjust to rapid social change.

Although social conflict can be an important source of frustration, most of the conflicts we experience in our daily lives are internal conflicts. Psychologists have identified three different categories of internal conflict.

The first of these may be viewed as a conflict between two or more very appealing choices. A simple example is the decision one must make in choosing dessert at a favorite restaurant. Let's suppose you are torn between indulging in the house specialty—apple pie a la mode—and the waiter's suggestion—coconut creme pie. Both choices have many positive features; both are very appealing to you. Such a conflict is referred to as an approach-approach conflict, since either alternative would be pleasant for you.

To solve the approach-approach conflict, you must consider a number of factors. Perhaps the piece of apple pie is considerably more expensive than that of the coconut creme; maybe one of the desserts is much larger than the other; maybe you just had coconut creme yesterday. By closely considering the various attributes of the two choices you may be able to successfully settle the approach-approach conflict.

Another type of conflict results from the necessity of choosing between two unpleasant alternatives. Do you go to the dentist or do you continue to have toothaches? Do you pay taxes or go to jail? Do you spend the weekend finalizing that important business deal or do you risk losing it on Monday? The conflict that results is an avoidance-avoidance conflict. As in the approach-approach situation, avoidance-avoidance conflicts can only be resolved by careful consideration of the long-term effects of each potential choice. You may finally decide that the prospects of a continuing toothache are much more unpleasant than a trip to the dentist. A more difficult decision may be finally realizing that breaking off an unhappy relationship with a lover may be less unpleasant than the continuation of an existing interpersonal struggle. Obviously, the more important the decision, the more difficult the resolution of the conflict.

Finally, at times we must make a choice that has both pleasant and unpleasant consequences. The same choice is both attractive and unattractive. Choosing to commit oneself to a professional career, such as medicine, for example, has many worthwhile rewards but it also involves a great deal of hard work. A second piece of pie would be very tasty but would also contribute a large number of calories to your diet.

This type of conflict is termed an approach-avoidance conflict. It can be the most difficult of all to resolve, since it involves weighing and comparing differing qualities—apples versus oranges, good against bad.

Conflict Resolution and Emotional Stability

The ability to successfully resolve difficult conflicts is a necessary feature of emotional maturity. The person who lives in a constant state of conflict, who is indecisive and uncertain, is usually characterized by anxiety and frustration. Much of the evidence linking conflict to psychological ills such as neurosis has been obtained through laboratory studies of animals.

For many years, scientists have known how to induce mental disturbance in animals such as rats, cats, and dogs. A common technique involves placing the animal in conflict, for instance, in an approach-avoidance situation. In a typical experiment, food serves as both a pleasant and unpleasant choice: the food will satisfy the animal's hunger, but touching it will give the animal an electric shock. The animal is thus forced into a state of conflict. The typical cat or dog placed in this conflict situation reacts in a dramatic fashion. For months after the conflict situation has been removed, previously quiet cats tend to be tense and nervous, sweating, trembling frequently, with raised blood pressure and irregular breathing. Other cats lose their tameness, becoming vicious and aggressive and attacking other cats in their cage. For all intents and purposes, the conflict situation produces a "mental breakdown" in the cats.

Psychologists have compared the conflict behavior of animals to that of human beings. Indeed, all of us have experienced the tenseness and anxiety resulting from indecision. When the choice to be made is a very important one, such as a career decision or the choice of a mate, and the alternatives are about equal in value, conflict can produce extreme emotional crises in otherwise healthy individuals. The ability to resolve conflicts, to assess the value of alternatives, to examine both present and future consequences of decisions is a very important part of mental health.

What is the process by which conflict produces emotional malfunctioning? Tension is created and if it is not released, it is expressed as anxiety. Humans in conflict, like the neurotic cats, react to tension build-up by becoming nervous, moody, and worried. If the anxiety is severe, the body reacts by tightening muscles, increasing heart rate and perspiration output, and changing breathing patterns.

Anxiety, like physical pain, is a signal that something is wrong; it indicates an internal conflict that needs to be resolved. It is a warning that you must now take some action to reduce conflict.

RX Prescription: Resolving conflict.

The prescription for conflict resolution is a simple one: you must learn to make decisions and stick by them. Whether your conflict is a major one or a minor one, it can be resolved on a conscious level. By carefully examining the alternatives that are the source of conflict, by weighing pros and cons, and by formulating a plan of action, you can make an informed choice that will put an end to your conflict situation and free your mind of the tension and anxiety arising from it.

Very few of us go through even a week of our lives without experiencing some degree of anxiety. But the brief periods of anxiety that beset the normal individual are hardly comparable to the intense and long-lasting years which mark the onset of neurosis.

Stress

Stress is the spice of life, there is no way of avoiding it. You are constantly being challenged to resist and adapt to changing external influences. Interestingly, it is completely irrelevant whether the agent or situation provoking stress is pleasant or unpleasant; the signs within us are the same. Even while fully relaxed and asleep you are under stress: your heart must continue to pump blood, your intestines to digest last night's dinner, your muscles to move your chest to permit respiration.

Contrary to popular prejudice, we must not—and indeed cannot—avoid stress. But we can meet it efficiently and channel it positively by learning more about its mechanisms and by adjusting our lifestyles accordingly.

When we say someone is under stress, we actually mean under excessive stress—distress. Each one of us has an optimal stress level. It is not the external event, but each individual's reaction to it, that is important. To keep stress from becoming distress, we must experience stress in specific amounts and situations, and for a finite length of time. Distress often results from prolonged or unvaried stress, or from frustration.

188

What are the different types of stress, and how do our bodies react to them?

Acute environmental stress occurs when a person reacts to a threatening event in the environment. The body reacts specifically: signals from the brain stimulate the autonomic nervous systems (over which you have no conscious control) which release powerful hormones to gear the body for action. The resulting "fight or flight" syndrome includes a set of reactions that are like vestigial tails; they are distant echoes of the way we once were. These reactions are: increases in rate and strength of heart beat; constrictions of blood vessels and increase in blood pressure; acceleration of blood sugar and fatty acids; dilation of nostrils and bronchi; increase in muscle tension; and retraction of the eyeballs and dilation of the pupils. All these speed the person's reactions and ready him to face the oncoming danger—whether it is fighting or running away. Fatty acids in the bloodstream fuel the muscles and make the blood clot more quickly if a wound is present. When there is no struggle these fatty acids are left circulating and may convert into cholesterol deposits. In fact, repeated environmental stress can be a major cause of atherosclerosis and related troubles, if no physical movement is involved to burn up the fatty acids produced. Moreover continual encounter with stress situations may result in constant high blood pressure.

Acute psychological stress is the result of incidents which have great impact on a person's life, mainly those involving conflict and change.

You may be in a state of conflict with another person, or with an abstract, such as time. Conflict produces emotions of anger or anxiety, which are often accompanied by the automatic physical changes of the fight or flight syndrome. For modern man these changes are usually as physically inappropriate as those arising from environmental effects, and so the same physically damaging results can occur.

The acute psychological stress we undergo when faced

with major change, however, involves no fight or flight syndrome. Although the process is not fully understood, recent research indicates that the common response to change is physical illness: people who have experienced dramatically stressful change typically get ill—over 75 percent within a year of the event, in one recent study.

Chronic environmental stress occurs when the physical conditions of a person's surroundings are unpleasant: a cramped and noisy working setting; a demand for constant alertness and readiness on the job. The body reacts in these situations with what has been named the General Adaptation Syndrome: a long-term adaptation to the presence of stress. This response tends to create permanent high blood pressure, as well as high blood cholesterol levels. Eventually the person feels exhausted both physically and mentally. Resistance to disease, or simply the desire to go on, breakdown, and physical, mental, and psychosomatic illness occur.

The effects of chronic psychological stress depend more on the individual—his characteristics and personality—than on the events. Someone promoted above his ability might be unaware of his limitations and tackle the new position happily and cheerfully. On the other hand, someone in a position well within his ability might work under constant pressure and tension. He might underestimate his capabilities; he may want a promotion; or this may simply be his way of working. The two personality types, in fact, have been contrasted by researchers who indicate that the latter type has intense ambition, competitive drive, and a sense of urgency, and is more prone to heart disease, although no satisfactory proof has yet been obtained; while the other has a contented, unhurried personality. The high correlation between ambitious people and heart disease is thought to occur because of high cholesterol and blood pressure levels.

Chronic psychological stress can also end in some form of illness, especially if constant tension is manifested as unpleasant exhaustion. If a person is trying to escape deep psychic conflicts by rushing through life, the process is less likely to end in illness. But it is more likely that psychic balance eventually collapses as outside events force hidden conflicts to the surface. These conflicts, such as social or sexual fears, then expose themselves in neurosis or other mental illness.

Anxiety is the name for illness that has its underlying cause in psychological stress. Butterflies in the stomach, eyestrain, tight jaw muscles, stiff neck, chin jutting out, biting or grinding teeth, sweating palms or cold hands, irritability, high pulse rate, irregular shallow breathing or sighing respiration, tight strained voice, are all signs of tension mounting within a person. If sustained long enough, these can result in real illnesses such as constipation and indigestion, dermatitis, hair loss, migraine, ulcers, essential hypertension, and stress symptoms in specific organs (such as heart pains and heart beat irregularities).

The questions for psychologists are: why does stress cause ulcers, high blood pressure, headaches, and other psychophysiological disorders in some people and not in others? What kinds of stress produce what kinds of disorders?

Genetic factors, earlier illnesses, and diet may selectively disrupt a particular organ system, which may then become weak and vulnerable to stress. And there are differences, probably genetically determined, in the ways in which individuals respond. Someone reacting to stress with secretion of stomach acid will be more vulnerable to ulcers, and someone reacting to stress with blood pressure elevation will be more susceptible to essential hypertension.

Anxiety, tension produced by frustration, anger, and depression, are the common causes of psychosomatic illness. Some people might respond with an overproduction of pepsinogen, a secretion of the stomach's gastric glands, and develop an ulcer. Others might secrete greater amounts of norepinephrine, which ultimately results in the retention of sodium in the walls of the arteries. The sodium causes arterial walls to overrespond to normal nerve impulses, causing them to restrict, producing hypertension. Still others might respond with asthma; a narrowing of the respiratory airways brought on by the chemical changes stress can produce.

RX Prescription: How to deal with the tension that leads to stress.

1. Get rid of that sense of urgency by substituting excellence and value for quantity and size. Learn to appreciate —nature, music, reading, personal relationships—instead of acquiring things. Develop your inner life and a strong system of values and beliefs that you can draw on when change inevitably comes.

2. Make deposits in your store of confidence; you'll also need to draw on it one day.

3. Put priorities on your time and energy. Don't squander them.

4. Learn to say no: when you say yes to something you don't want to do, you put yourself into the middle of a stressful situation.

5. Give each thing you do your undivided attention. You will finish it sooner, more pleasurably, less nervously. Live each moment in the present; don't always look toward the future.

6. Slow yourself down with deep breathing and relaxation techniques; leave time in the day for self-contemplation.

7. Try to work in a peaceful environment.

8. If you are angry, work it off physically, get rid of it. Clean the house or prune the trees.

9. Divide huge blocks of work into more manageable segments that you work on one at a time. But if a task is too big, don't do it.

10. Make lists.

11. Use odd bits of time, like commuting or waiting in line, to do small tasks.

12. Watch your diet: ideally, eliminate all caffeine, and cut down drastically on sugar (be sure to read ingredients on boxes of prepared foods; many, like meat stretchers, packaged lasagna, vegetables, contain sugar). On the other hand, protein should be part of every meal because it slows down the release of sugar and energy and therefore smooths wide fluctuations in your body chemistry. The B-complex vitamins are very helpful in relieving stress.

RX Prescription: Play in work.

Ignore these cherished slogans: "There is more in life than just work"; "You should work to live, not live to work." These sound pretty convincing, but are they really? Don't try to avoid work; aim to find the kind of occupation which, for you, is closest to play. The best way to avoid undue stress is to select an environment (spouse, boss, social group) which complements your innate preferences, and invest your time and energy in work that you like and respect. Only in this way can you eliminate the need for constant adaptation that is the major cause of stress.

Sleep

Lack of sleep has as severe an effect as lack of food. A person kept awake for long periods becomes increasingly disoriented and both mentally and physically exhausted. Death usually occurs after a period of ten days of total sleep deprivation. But what is sleep? We still know very little about it, and each discovery unveils yet another aspect of this very complex process.

We do not sleep merely to satisfy the body's demand for rest. In that case lying down would be adequate. Sleep enables us to relax our muscles and "rest" the brain. Yet even in deepest sleep the brain functions.

Sleep falls into two main stages: orthodox or phase IV sleep, and paradoxical sleep. Orthodox sleep is characterized by a lowering of the heart beat, blood pressure, and the metabolic rate. Breathing is regular but slow. It is the deepest sleep and the most physically restorative. In light orthodox sleep, movement occurs: up to 40 changes in position a night. However, in deep orthodox sleep both muscles and brain are at their most relaxed. There is no movement and the electrical

194

activity of the brain is markedly different from the waking state. It is during this sleep stage that the output of growth hormones and protein production is stepped up; the body repairs itself and dead cells are replaced.

Paradoxical or REM (rapid eye movement) sleep is the stage in which dreams occur. Breathing and heart beat become irregular, eyes move behind closed eyelids. The electrical activity of the brain is similar to that of the waking state. Although movement may occur, the muscles are often as relaxed as in orthodox sleep, to prevent the acting out of dreams, it is thought.

A normal sleep pattern begins with light orthodox sleep lasting about 30 minutes, followed by deep orthodox sleep. This first period of deep sleep is usually the longest of the night, lasting about an hour. The sleeper then advances through light sleep to the first period of paradoxical sleep, about one and a half hours after falling asleep. This cycle recurs about five times during a typical sleep of seven to eight hours. However, as the night progresses the period of deep sleep becomes shorter until after about three hours it might no longer be reached. Instead, the periods of light orthodox and paradoxical sleep become correspondingly longer. Paradoxical sleep occupies about 20 percent of an adult's sleeping time.

When given the chance to make up lost orthodox sleep on "rebound" nights, subjects' percentage of that sleep will be much greater than normal.

In experiments where people were continually awakened and thereby deprived of the dreaming stage of sleep, on "recovery nights," instead of dreaming 20 percent of the night, they dream for 30, 40, or even 50 percent of their sleep time. As phase IV sleep is restorative, REM sleep seems to be important in terms of problem solving. Several years ago in an experiment described in the medical literature, two groups of subjects were shown a grisly horror movie before they went to sleep, and then allowed to sleep in the laboratory. Half of the group weren't allowed to dream, while the control group was allowed to dream and awakened at random. Through various measurements taken the next morning, such as galvanic skin response, anxiety was measured and found to be much higher in those who had been dream deprived. Apparently the people who had been allowed to dream worked through some of their anxiety by incorporating into their dreams some of the frightening portions of the movie.

Often before someone has a psychotic break—a manic-depressive psychosis, or a schizophrenic episode—a warning signal can be severe insomnia. A younger person who has been sleeping well and suddenly begins sleeping poorly should immediately seek professional help.

Chronic insomnia occurs in as much as 15 percent of the population. It is real, but has no proven cause and can only be treated symptomatically. Transient insomnia, arising from poor sleeping conditions, psychological stress, or a medical disorder, usually disappears when the conditions causing it are remedied. When patients with insomnia who report they haven't slept in days or months are hospitalized and observed by a nursing staff, it is usually discovered that they do sleep—often for long periods. However, high voltage, slow wave sleep—the phase IV sleep that normally takes place in the early part of the night—is diminished. In short, the patient gets more sleep than he believes he does but the quality of that sleep is poor.

There are two major types of insomnia. One afflicts people who can't get to sleep, who go to bed at ten o'clock and lie staring into the darkness until one or two o'clock in the morning. Usually those people have either a neurotic, pre-psychotic, or psychotic illness, and psychotherapy or counselling is the best treatment. These subjects usually have problems that need to be solved, and no chemical can do that for them.

The second major sleep disorder affects those who wake up at three or four A.M. and can't get back to sleep. These are generally people with classical kinds of depression, accompanied by sadness, crying spells, somber moods. Even if they are not subjectively aware of their depression they are usually conscious of apathy, lessening of former interests, loss of sexual libido. For these subjects treatment is important and usually consists of antidepressive medication along with psychotherapy.

To date, science has not developed any definite theory to explain the mechanisms triggering sleep. An answer could be the key to a cure for insomnia. Several hypotheses have been postulated: a reduction in the amount of oxygen reaching the brain; a decrease in the number of impulses reaching the conscious centers; a chemical process in the brain; or the repeated promptings of a conditioned response. It is also known that certain cell groups within the brain bring about sleep when stimulated, while others cause the sleeper to wake. However, the exact nature and function of these cells has not been ascertained.

RX Prescription: A new sleeping pill.

For occasional simple insomnia, many experts recommend increased exercise during the day, and nutritional aids such as calcium-magnesium tablets. The old-fashioned glass of milk at bedtime, or when awakening during the night, can indeed have a soothing effect on the nerves.

In a recent study, insomnia sufferers passed up their regular pills in favor of an experimental glass of milk. They fell asleep in about half the time and slept an average of 45 minutes longer. In addition to the protein in milk which raises blood sugar levels (low blood sugar can be a cause of wakefulness), it was discovered that a natural ingredient in milk—the amino acid tryptophan—acted as the necessary tranquilizer. Tryptophan is the pivotal ingredient in the formation of serotonin.

Depression

It has been estimated that a quarter of our adult population suffers from depression acute enough to demand treatment, according to Nathan S. Kline, M.D., director of the Rockland Research Institute, and leading authority on depression. This amounts to about thirty million people, making it not only the most widespread psychological disorder, but also one of the most common of all serious medical conditions. Dr. Kline has also stated that depression is the most undertreated of all major diseases.

Everyone has periods of sadness, ranging from the "blues" one feels after losing a job or ending a love affair, to the deep sorrow experienced after a traumatic loss or major tragedy. Such normal and usually temporary states are not the same as clinically defined depression. Many people experience severe depression and suffer through it without realizing that it is a treatable condition, says Dr. William E. Bunney, Jr., of the National Institute of Mental Health. For yourself or those close to you, it is important to know and recognize the symptoms: feelings of worthlessness, helplessness, and apathy; a desire to stay away from others; difficulty sleeping, fatigue; loss of appetite leading to weight loss; loss of sexual libido; change in activity level, becoming either lethargic or agitated; thoughts of death and suicide.

Depression occurs in all age groups and is not infrequent in young adults. Most often it occurs in passive, insecure, and oversensitive people who are unable or unwilling to retaliate against aggression or openly express anger.

Many depressed patients are sad, cry frequently, and complain of feeling unhappy or "blue." But beyond mere sadness, they may also lose the ability to feel pleasure. In this stage, called anhedonia, the feelings that usually make life worth living are absent and the ideas, activities, friendships, and events that usually bring pleasure seem empty or hollow. Pessimism about the future is another feature of depressive illness. During the sad times of life, people are generally comforted by the thoughts of a happier future time. However, for many depressed patients, the future looks as bleak and barren as the present.

Low self-esteem is a hallmark of depression. Most people retain a good concept of their personal value through periods of sadness but depressed patients often deny their past accomplishments or feel unworthy of their current achievements. The feeling of worthlessness combines with pessimism to rob depressed patients of their motivation to carry on with their jobs or their interpersonal relationships. In many instances, the first sign of depression is the increasing difficulty that a person has in executing everyday tasks that he or she would usually handle quite easily.

There are two major categories of depression: unipolar and bipolar. Bipolar depression involves alternating "highs" and "lows" and is more commonly known as manic depression. Depressive or "low" episodes are usually psychotic and are characterized by hallucinations, delusions, and paranoid ideas. Manic or "high" states can involve extreme agitation, aggression, constant restlessness and talking, and grandiosity.

An interesting aspect of manic depression is that it possesses a genetically linked component. In studies with nonidentical twins, there is a 12 percent chance that if one twin is manic depressive, the other twin will be as well. With identical twins, the probability that the other twin will be similarly afflicted rises to 70 percent. There is no question that this malady involves a biological, possibly biochemical, abnormality which can be triggered by a variety of environmental factors.

Unipolar depression is recurrent depression without manias and is characterized by constant "lows."

These two broad categories can be further subdivided into other classifications: neurotic or psychotic; exogenous or endogenous. Psychotic depression is defined by the presence of delusions and the greater severity of symptoms. Exogenous means "originating outside the body" and is applied to depression that has an environmental cause. Endogenous, "originating within the body" applies to disorders having an internal physical cause.

Another recent development in the treatment of depression is cognitive therapy. Cognitive theories of depression suggest that a person's beliefs and thoughts influence his emotional state. Aaron Beck, a pioneer in this field, found that his depressed patients tended to distort whatever happened to them in the direction of self-blame, or to magnify them into catastrophy. He describes several logical errors committed by depressed people in interpreting reality: 1) Arbitrary influence: a conclusion drawn in the absence of sufficient evidence or any evidence at all. For example, a person concludes that he is worthless because it is raining the day he is hosting an outdoor cocktail party. 2) Selective abstraction: a conclusion drawn on the basis of only one of many elements in a situation. A worker blames himself entirely for the failure of a product or function even though he is only one of many people who have produced it. 3) Overgeneralization: an overall, sweeping conclusion drawn on the basis of a single, perhaps trivial, event. A student regards his poor performance in a single class on one particular day as final proof of his worthlessness and stupidity. 4) Magnification and minimization: gross errors in evaluating performance. A person believes that he has completely ruined his car (magnification) when he sees that there is a light scratch on the rear fender; a person still believes himself worthless (minimization) in spite of a succession of praiseworthy achievements.

Learning theorists postulate that depression occurs when an accustomed reinforcement is withdrawn. The loss of a job or a loved one removes the positive reinforcement associated with the activity or person. The result is a reduction in activity and depressionlike symptoms. Lack of reinforcement reduces still further the activities and expression of qualities that might be rewarded. Both activities and rewards decrease in a vicious circle.

Another way of looking at depression is defining it as learned helplessness. Although anxiety, a state of heightened mental and physical activity, is the initial response to a stressful situation, if the stress continues indefinitely, the person comes to believe that his environment is out of his control. One cannot act to reduce suffering or gain gratification; one loses hope and initiative. Anxiety is replaced by depression.

From this brief discussion, it is clear that there are many different schools of thought concerning depression, and few agree on the proper treatment. Those oriented toward the exogenous or environmental theory of depression tend to rely on traditional methods of psychotherapy—talking things out with a doctor in a clinical setting; reliving and resolving the traumas of childhood.

Those favoring the endogenous theory rely heavily on drug therapy, hoping to counteract chemical insufficiencies and thereby alleviate the depression. These doctors have developed the theory that we have dealt with throughout the EMM, namely that the neurotransmitters, serotonin and norepinephrine, are involved in depression. They facilitate the transmission of "messages" between brain cells. A decrease in either could cause a depression. Although these theories remain unproved, the treatment devised to meet this hypothesis remains standard—use of drugs that reestablish the chemical levels in the brain, such as lithium, Elavil, or Tofranil.

It takes several weeks for antidepressant drugs to work; while there may be uncomfortable side effects in the beginning, the body must be given the chance to adjust. The drugs must be continued until the administering doctor suspends them, even if the patient feels better. One should not feel weak or guilty about taking medication for a long period of time if it is needed.

Ongoing research in the field of depression continues to pay a great deal of attention to physiological causes.

Electrolyte metabolism is now being investigated as a possible physiological cause of depression. Electrolytes play a central role in the functioning of the nervous system. Two of the most important of these are sodium and potassium chloride. The level of intracellular sodium has been found to be elevated in psychotically depressed patients. A corresponding decrease in the level of extracellular sodium has also been determined. The result of this disturbed distribution of electrolytes is to make the depressed person's nervous system hyperexcitable. He responds more quickly and forcefully to sensory stimuli even though overt behavior seems retarded and lethargic.

Dr. Robert Greenblatt, Professor Emeritus of the Medical College of Georgia and world authority on endocrinology, believes that hormones can be of significant help in postmenopausal depression. There is a great deal of anxiety at this time of life when the last child has usually left home. It can produce classic depression known as the "empty nest" syndrome. Many women respond to large doses of pure, non-synthetic estrogen and experience dramatic relief from depression, just as large doses of natural testosterone can be effective in treating male climacteric depression.

One of the major contributions to American psychiatry of the past generation, lithium carbonate, an ordinary mineral salt, can reverse the tendency toward bouts of bipolar depression; there is evidence that it is effective in unipolar depression as well.

The newest discovery in biochemical treatment of depression is the effect of a substance we discussed in an earlier chapter: tryptophan, an amino acid and precursor of serotonin, found in proteins such as meat, eggs, milk.

In tests at the West Suffolk Hospital in England, tryptophan was used on nine depressed patients and an antidepressant drug, imipramine, was given to seven others. Both groups showed dramatic improvement over a four-week period, indicating tryptophan was as effective as the prescription drug and users did not risk harmful side effects. Similar results were reported from tests in hospitals in Denmark, Finland, Norway, and Sweden. A study in London found tryptophan-Vitamin B_3 (nicotinamide) supplements superior to convulsive shock therapy in treating depression.

It is probably safe to assume that both physiological and environmental factors play a role in depression. Biological depression affects one's self-image, thereby increasing stress and exacerbating the biological problem, and creating a vicious cycle that often seems difficult to break.

Whatever treatment is used, depression must be considered a serious illness and should never be ignored. The National Institute of Mental Health has produced a form listing common symptoms of clinical depression. If you have noted any of these symptoms, it is probably wise to consult a doctor.

• Dysphoric mood: prominent and persistent with feelings of depression, hopelessness, emptiness, and so forth.

• Clusters of symptoms, including at least five of the following:

Appetite disturbance (decrease or increase).

Sleep disturbance (decrease or increase).

Loss of energy.

Psychomotor retardation (or agitation).

Loss of interest in usually pleasurable activities.

Slowed thinking, decreased ability to concentrate or re-member.

Self-blame and inappropriate guilt.

Recurrent thoughts of death or suicide.

(Duration of the above, at least two weeks. Impaired functioning.)

Depression and Doubt

In order to grow you must minimize certain unpleasant feelings in your life, such as doubt, dread, and depression. All of us experience these emotions but they cannot become perva-sive, or take over our lives. There are ways to deal with them if you are willing to recognize and understand them. As you grow toward self-actualization, you will tend to experience fewer and fewer persistent unpleasant feelings.

Self-doubt is one of the most debilitating emotions we can encounter. Many people are unsure about their physical appearance; they consider themselves unattractive, ugly, and therefore unlovable. They avoid interpersonal relationships be-cause they feel that others cannot possibly enjoy their com-pany. Similar self-doubts arise about intelligence, creativity, athletic ability, and job skills. Excessive self-doubt, in gen-eral, comes from a feeling that other people will not find you acceptable in some way; this feeling leads you not to accept yourself. Understanding and forgiving others their frailties is one way to avoid self-doubt; you will discover that your own weaknesses and fears are not unique. Allowing yourself to be loved and prized by someone is another way to escape exces-sive self-doubt; to be accepted by someone else makes it easier for you to accept yourself and by accepting yourself, it's easier to accept others.

Dread is a nonspecific emotion similar to anxiety. You feel afraid, but you are not sure why. You become nervous, high-strung, restless, and irritable. A persistent feeling of dread is a message that you should relax, reduce the pressures in your life, and try to resolve some of your conflicts.

Your problems and conflicts can sometimes be eased by talking to other people about them. As you listen to yourself, you may gain some insights. The feedback of other people may also give you a new perspective. Expressing your feelings to other people often in itself reduces the tension that you feel, as long as you don't *only* talk about problems.

We have already considered depression in some detail. We are using the term here to define the relatively mild depression we all experience as a normal part of life. The prescriptions below should help to alleviate this problem.

RX Prescription: Action.

Action is a basic cure for depression—get involved in things around you. Take an interest in other people's lives and by so doing, you will take an interest in your own life. Your involvement does not have to be great. Join a club, volunteer in a community clinic or agency, start a project—rouse yourself out of the doldrums.

By minimizing these negative feelings, you can open yourself to psychological growth and take charge of your life.

RX Prescription: Knowing, feeling, exploring.

Knowing

Knowledge fosters feelings of security. When you have mastered a particular skill, or understand another person, you feel good about yourself. Knowledge presupposes learning, and learning depends on involvement with life and with others.

Self-understanding cannot easily be achieved in isolation; other people define us to ourselves. Other people consistently mirror us when they react to us, so self-understanding depends upon your relationship with others. As others accept you you accept yourself. Self-understanding and self-acceptance are experiences of growth that make possible a state of self-actualization.

Feeling

Experiences that confirm who you are, are healthy experiences. Being loved by someone is a validation of you; it means that someone accepts you and values you for those things they know about you. To be loved helps you to know, accept, and value yourself.

The ability to give love is also a sign of growth. In order to love another you must be able to open yourself both to intimacy and criticism, and to be willing to take a deep interest in another person. Love helps you to gain faith in your own powers.

Exploring

Living is a constant exploration of the world. When you actively do things, you experience your self, your power, your limits. When you become intensely involved in something outside yourself—a job, hobby, cause, or another person—you diminish self-consciousness and develop feelings of competence, direction, and significance. You begin to experience a kind of self-transcendence. Exploration is a growth experience.

To know you must be open to change. To feel you must give. To explore you must act. Make these three words a part of your working emotional vocabulary.

The One
and Only You

Astrologers attribute the differences between us to the influence of heavenly bodies, and the direction and fortune of our lives to the configuration of the stars at the moment of our birth. But our real stars, of course, are the egg cell and the sperm cell that joined to bring us into existence. At the moment of conception, a confluence of genes occurred that would never again be duplicated. Chance and environment began to model us, and slowly, that unique conglomeration of cells, endowed with the incredible miracle of consciousness, began in turn to model itself; to think in a certain way, to have opinions, to imagine, act, and react in a certain way. Those processes are guided within each of us by chemicals of widely varying composition, which direct and modify our appetites, emotions, growth, energy, drive, intelligence, and stability. And those chemicals, in turn, are programmed by a brain that is unique to each of us, not only in its structure, its surface area, the depth of its convolutions, its weight, the relative size of its parts, but in the way it interprets those perceptions. The physical differences innate in all of us are just structural,

207

tangible, weighable manifestations of the intangible, ephemeral, all-important quality that is our individuality, our mind, our personality.

All of the preceding pages have been devoted to leading you toward an ideal state of emotional stability, allowing you to predict and control your reactions to problems both minor and traumatic. Repeatedly we've reminded you of the energy you can save—ending arguments quickly and satisfactorily, avoiding depression, expressing yourself, defending your beliefs, minimizing anxiety, not dwelling on the past nor fretting about the future. That energy can then be directed toward other, positive, forward-looking aspects of your life. Activities whose values are intrinsic and will provide feedback, brightening, and enriching the routine of your life with the inner glow, the stream of energy and happiness that comes from being completely immersed in what you are doing. Artists, composers, surgeons, mountain climbers, athletes all experience this kind of ecstasy when they lose their awareness of self, of their problems, and become one with their task, their creative activity. How can you make your life more like this? By sharpening your skills, matching them to your undertakings, developing total awareness of the moment and living in it. So much time is wasted digging up the past or dreading the future, instead of living out the present, using the unique qualities that you have to their utmost, making them work for you to create something beyond yourself, so that work becomes play, and play, pure delight.

What we've been leading up to is sweeping out the shop so you can get to work using the machinery in it. And don't say "I'm just not creative."

Everyone is creative and we all generate creative ideas. We create our own internal and external environments, our fantasies, dreams, visions, ideas. More often than not they are original, not just as works of art but as solutions to problems.

But creativity means something much deeper, more general, more innate than what an artist, an architect, or a scientist does. Remember two things: man is earth's only creator; and creativity means *to bring into being, to cause to exist.* In other words, creation is a profoundly and uniquely human attribute. We now know that animals have emotions, and even language; but they don't create. And it is as simple and as universal as it is human. It is as necessary to us as laughter or love. Creativity is a four-year-old choosing an orange crayon instead of a red one; it is the prize hybrid rose of a lonely middle-aged bachelor; it is our landing on the moon. It has nothing to do with intelligence, everything to do with ingenuity. It has nothing to do with art, everything to do with artfulness. It is putting together elements in a new way—new for everyone, or just for you.

Creative people—whether creative in their work, their relationships, or their play—are imaginative, independent, individualistic, sensitive, committed, self-accepting, spontaneous, impulsive, and in their independent attitudes, willing to take risks.

RX *Prescription:* Take the chance.

If you experience difficulty thinking something through, conceptualizing it, your problem is probably partly emotional. You have to put yourself on the line when you *do* think something through; you must expose your imperfections. So rather than exposing yourself, you simply avoid conceptualizing. Get it over with. Take the chance. Get past it, and get on with your work. There can be no change without risks. Don't be afraid to make mistakes. We all do.

Now apply some of these novel ways of examining problems to your own life:

RX *Prescription:* Working.

1. What do you want to do? Be clear, list up to five points to define your goal as exactly as possible.
2. Where do you want to do it?

3. What are your skills? List five, in order of proficiency.

4. What are the organizations or individuals that might need your abilities? Seek out the person who is in the position to evaluate your abilities and *act*.

5. Use a unique approach to gain attention. Be clear and insightful in your presentation.

"To be creative means to experience life in one's own way, to perceive from one's own person, to draw upon one's own resources, capacities, roots. It means facing life directly and honestly. When a person's involvement in a situation is based on appearances, expectations, or the standards of others; when he acts in a conventional manner, or according to prescribed roles and functions, when he is concerned with status and approval; his growth as a creative self is impaired. When the individual is conforming, following, imitating, being like others, he moves increasingly in the direction of self-alienation. . . . Gradually the conforming person loses touch with himself, with his own real feelings."

RX Prescription: The creative climate.

Several important conditions necessary for creativity to flourish have been isolated by Carl Rogers, noted American proponent of client-centered therapy. Have the crash program's exercises brought you any closer to the first three conditions, which must originate within you? And can you alter your environment to meet the last three conditions, making it more hospitable for yourself as well as for those close to you?

1. Openness to experience. Instead of perceiving in predetermined categories, the individual is aware of experiences falling outside the usual categories. Rather than the perception "Trees are green," the particular perception "This tree is brown and yellow" is a possibility. To be

open to experience is to be sensitive to things as they really are, rather than according to convention or prior expectation. To be open to experience is to deter closure or labeling; to postpone a conclusion about the nature of your experience until the evidence is all in. If you are open to experience, you are able to experience me as I really am, rather than jumping to conclusions about me on the basis of your prior expectations.

2. Internal locus of evaluation. Instead of deciding what is good or appropriate on the basis of external standards established by others, the creative person uses an internal standard of evaluation. A creative individual strives to satisfy his own expectations, rather than someone else's.

3. Ability to toy with elements and concepts. Instead of taking ideas and concepts as given, a creative person plays with them by changing the relationships and juggling the elements into different orders. This spontaneous play yields new and unusual combinations of ideas; by exploring these new combinations, the creative person is able to see problems in fresh ways.

4. Unconditional acceptance. The worth of the individual is not dependent upon his performance. He is unconditionally accepted and valued as a person by those significant other persons in his life. His acceptance is not conditional upon his achievement or good behavior.

5. Absence of external evaluation. The individual and his behavior are not continually being judged and evaluated by others. He is allowed to develop his own independent standards.

6. Empathetic understanding. The individual, his experiences and feelings, are understood by the significant other people around him in the world. They are able to understand his point of view and sympathetically share in his private world.*

* This material, adapted from Carl Rogers, is taken from *Psychology: An Introduction to Human Behavior*, Morris Holland, D. C. Heath & Co.

RX Prescription: Checklist for new ideas.

Developing Numbers 1, 2, and 3 above a little further, use this list (adapted from one used in the Engineering Design Division at Stanford) when you have to find a solution to a problem. Try to remember as much of it as you can; it will prove useful whether you are dealing with an emotional relationship problem, or a creative impasse between you and yourself.

Can I put this to other uses, leaving it as it is, or modifying it?

Can I adapt this idea or situation? Can I copy another one? Is there something in the past I can refer to?

How can I change it? Its meaning, its physical form, its sensory qualities?

How can I make it grow? In terms of size, time, frequency, strength, value, exaggeration?

How can I make it smaller? In terms of subtracting, condensing, lowering, omitting, streamlining, dividing, understanding?

What can I substitute? Who else, what else, what more, what other way, where else?

How can I rearrange? Reorder the parts, a different sequence, different cause and effect, change of pace?

How can I reverse? Turn things inside out, backwards, upside down, change around, consider opposites?

How can I combine? Combine units, blend, bring together?

RX Prescription: Taking a risk.

Another common emotional block to creativity is the fear of taking a risk. A good way of overcoming this fear is to list the possible negative consequences of your idea, from minor inconveniences to life-shaking catastrophes. By making and studying such a list you can trade your fear of the (once) unknown for cold hard analysis. Then you can make a decision based on real information.

The Healthy Person

After all of the analysis you've done over the last days, you probably feel that description should fit you. It probably won't, not yet. But you are headed in the right direction if you followed the 3-Day Crash Program, and have started on the Lifelong Maintenance Program; if you administer those prescriptions to yourself when you aren't feeling strong in a particular area.

A healthy person is a fully functioning person, one who is content, creative, socially effective. To live well one must grow, be involved, be able to weather change and overcome conflict.

RX Prescription: Your chart. (Based on the writings of Carl Rogers and Abraham Maslow.)

Make a chart every month or so, based on these 15 questions, to keep track of where you are, to remind you of areas that need work.

1. You feel good; most of the time you have a feeling of well-being.
2. You feel secure and safe; you are rarely anxious.
3. You have feelings of belonging and rootedness; you do not usually feel isolated or an outcast.
4. You feel loved and love-worthy; you rarely feel rejected, worthless, unlovable, or inferior.
5. You feel competent; you are relatively self-confident about your own abilities; you have self-esteem and self-respect.
6. You trust and you are open to your own feelings; you

are immediately aware of your feelings and can act on them; you can be spontaneous.

7. You have "peak experiences"—ecstatic, intensely satisfying moments when all seems vividly real.

8. You can do things; you function well.

9. You can do most of the things you want to do; you can take care of yourself.

10. You are committed to and intensely involved in some work or cause "outside of your own skin."

11. You can accept yourself and others; you can disclose yourself to others.

12. You can experience fully, without self-consciousness.

13. You can show both spontaneity and self-control.

14. You have the capacity for forming and maintaining intimate interpersonal relationships; you can love.

15. You can be self-directed; you are relatively independent from the expectations of others. You are creative.

A Word
About Cycles

Our emotions, like our lives, run in cycles. We are not the same today as we were yesterday; nonetheless it can safely be predicted that much of what we are today will be that way tomorrow.

Your emotions, your physical states, fluctuate, ebb and flow like the tides. The periodic rhythms of the menstrual cycle, the stresses of premenstrual tension, are matched by masculine cycles of hormonal fluctuation that are less widely acknowledged. Various bodily functions have cycles, known as circadian cycles that approximate the 24-hour day; your reactions, your efficiency, your moods vary widely throughout this cycle. Medications are more effective when given at one period of the day than at another; alcohol is more toxic, less tolerable if taken early in the morning. Fortunately, the cocktail hour comes at a point in the daily cycle when the body can most effectively tolerate alcohol.

Lunacy originally meant intermittent insanity which changed in intensity with the phases of the moon. Psychiatric hospitals have statistics demonstrating that patients are more disturbed during the full moon; crime records indicate arson, theft, and automobile accidents increase with the waxing of the moon.

Many little-known facts point up these cycles; there are 82 percent more hemorrhages in throat operations in the second quarter of the moon than at any other time. Signs of premature aging have been observed in experimental animals when their customary periods of darkness and light are inverted. Indications of this same aging have been recorded with airline pilots working on east-west flights. Everyone is familiar with the stressful effects of jet lag; after a lengthy flight many individuals take up to two weeks to return to normal, becoming dizzy with sleep at five P.M., staring at the ceiling at three A.M.

Most coronaries, most incidences of the onset of labor, occur in the early hours of the morning. Most babies are born between midnight and six A.M. More babies are born in March than any other month.

Peak body temperature and peak performance are related; both usually increase during the first three hours after awakening. Some researchers report that our mental performance tends to be best between two and four P.M., at its worst between two and four A.M. Temperature, respiration, pulse, blood pressure, blood sugar, hormone, and hemoglobin levels all show circadian variations.

The Greeks believed people's lives fluctuated in seven-year cycles; when Greek doctors deemed treatment was necessary, it was prescribed in three- or seven-day cycles.

Birds navigate by the sun with an internal mechanism that is much like a clock. Since we, too, have internal clocks which regulate our bodies, we can learn to observe and use them by keeping a diary charting our rhythmic fluctuations over a period of several weeks. We can thereby recognize that some of our periods of depression and anxiety are due to underlying physical patterns that are more the result of body chemistry and glandular functioning than the external events of our lives. We can become aware of our cycles of restlessness and irritability throughout the day; of the variations in our ability to concentrate. We seem to have roughly a ninety-minute cycle of wakefulness/sleepiness throughout our lives which can be disturbed by anxiety, illness, drugs. By becoming aware of this cycle in ourselves, we can anticipate drowsiness and take short naps or rests at the appropriate time, or fall asleep more easily on the right schedule. Such self-knowledge can also help us awaken from sleep. When we learn to listen to our inner rhythms we can not only program falling asleep and awakening at will, but we can anticipate our most efficient hours and plan our lives accordingly. Larks and owls —morning and night people—have different rhythms of metabolism and hormonal activity. Learn which you are, if you don't already know, and make your life pattern fit this natural inclination. We not only march to different drummers psychologically, but we have different physiological rhythms. Regular habits keep our lives in order—a sensible routine adapted to our own personal cycles, those circadian rhythms that influence the way we feel and behave.

Our metabolism varies with the circling hours. Breakfast is the meal that is most efficiently consumed. The often-heard advice about eating a large breakfast is sound, not only to provide more energy for the day, but for weight control. Unfortunately, most Americans consume 80 percent of their daily food intake after six P.M., when it has more of a tendency to pile up pounds.

Stress and emotional problems may distort sleeping patterns, cause desynchronization of body rhythms. The output of adrenal neurohormones is related to depression—its victims don't exhibit normal circadian hormone patterns. Even after depression is cured it often takes a long time before normal bodily rhythms reappear. Our minds act on our bodies and vice versa. What we think produces physical changes and these patterns may affect our emotions and our thought processes.

Appendix

To test the effectiveness of the Emotional Maintenance 3-Day Crash Program and the EMM Lifelong Maintenance Program, subjects were randomly assigned to one of two different groups. Half were assigned to the non-EMM (control) group, and half were assigned to the EMM (experimental) group. Subjects in both groups were asked to fill out the Emotional Maintenance Inventory (EMI)—measuring emotional stability—and tests measuring states of anxiety and depression three times during the course of the study—at the beginning of the study, three days after the beginning of the study, and again six months later. The EMM group was tested at the beginning of the study, put through the EMM 3-Day Crash Program, tested a second time, taught to use the EMM Lifelong Maintenance Program, and then tested again six months later. The non-EMM group did nothing more than fill out the tests at the beginning of the study, three days later, and again six months later. The non-EMM group did not participate in the EMM 3-Day Crash Program, nor were they taught the use of the Lifelong Maintenance Program.

By comparing the average anxiety, depression, and EMI scores of the non-EMM and EMM groups, we could measure the effectiveness of the Emotional Maintenance 3-Day Crash Program and the Lifelong Maintenance Program.

We expected the scores of the non-EMM group to remain relatively constant all three times they were tested, since they did not receive the EMM programs or any other therapy designed to increase emotional stability during the course of this study. If the EMM programs were effective, we expected to see a significant decrease in the EMM group's anxiety, depression, and EMI scores after the 3-Day Crash Program, and continued low scores after six months of the Lifelong Maintenance Program. Low scores indicate improvement—more emotional stability, less anxiety, and less depression.

Our findings, summarized in tables 1, 2, and 3 were quite striking. Initially we found that the average scores of both groups, the non-EMM (control) and EMM (experimental), were almost the same for the Emotional Maintenance Inventory (EMI) and the depression and anxiety tests. But when tested three days later, we found that on the average the EMM group, the group that took the EMM 3-Day Crash Program, scored significantly lower in feelings of anxiety, feelings of depression, and the EMI than did the non-EMM group, the group that did not take the 3-Day Crash Program. Look at figures 1, 2, and 3, and notice that all three scores of the non-EMM group remained relatively constant from the first testing to the second, while the scores of the EMM group showed a large decrease. In other words, after the EMM 3-Day Crash Program, the EMM group experienced significantly less anxiety, less depression, and more emotional stability than did the non-EMM group.

Looking at figures 1, 2, and 3 again, notice that when the subjects were tested again six months later, on all three measures—anxiety, depression, and EMI—the average scores of the non-EMM group, the group that *was not* taught the use of the EMM Lifelong Maintenance Program, again re-

TABLE 1: MEAN TEST SCORES BEFORE EMM CRASH PROGRAM

Group	Test Scores					Sex	N	Mean Age	Mean Education
	Anxiety		Depression		EMI				
	Mean	SD	Mean	SD	Mean				
Control	8.2	4.8	14.9	7.7	402	M F	30 30	32 35	18 16
Experimental	8.1	5.0	15.0	7.7	397	M F	34 30	33 36	17 16

TABLE 2: MEAN TEST SCORES AFTER 3 DAYS

Group	Test Scores					Sex	N
	Anxiety		Depression		EMI		
	Mean	SD	Mean	SD			
Control	7.9	4.2	15.1	7.8	389	M F	30 28
Experimental	6.2*	3.8	11.1*	5.2	335*	M F	28 32

*Significantly lower than control group: p < .05

TABLE 3: MEAN TEST SCORES AFTER 6 MONTHS

Group	Test Scores					Sex	N
	Anxiety		Depression		EMI		
	Mean	SD	Mean	SD			
Control	8.1	4.4	15.3	7.6	367	M F	20 26
Experimental	5.1*	3.1	9.2	4.8	217*	M F	25 28

*Significantly lower than control group: P < .05

FIG. 1: MEAN ANXIETY TEST SCORES

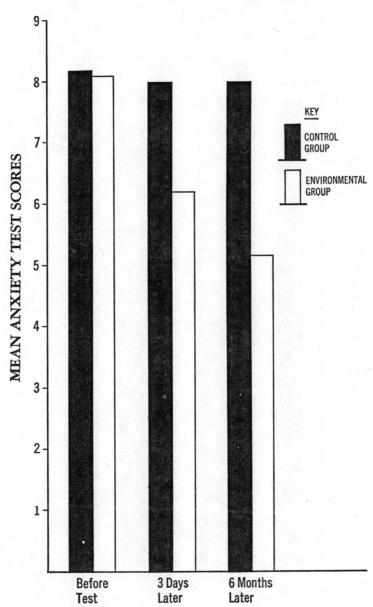

FIG. 2: MEAN DEPRESSION TEST SCORES

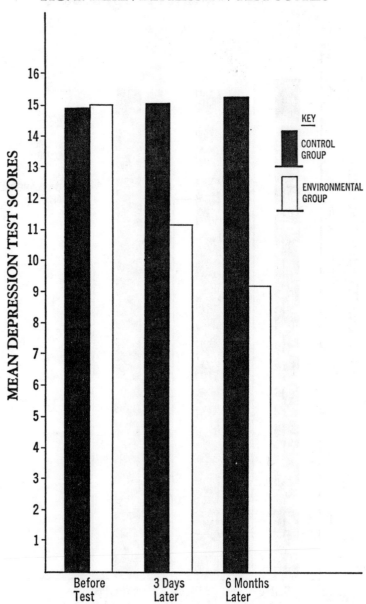

FIG. 3: MEAN EMI SCORES

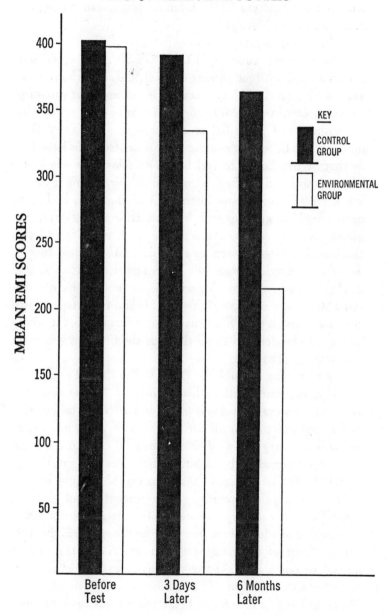

mained fairly constant while the EMM group, the group that *was* taught to use the EMM Lifelong Maintenance Program, decreased their scores again.

Six case studies follow:

One of our subjects, J.L., 37, male, was a businessman who had achieved success in his field during the last two years with a resulting large increase in income. But just prior to taking part in the EMM program he had begun to feel that his business and home life were starting to slip away from him; he felt he was beginning to lose control. He later told us that he had begun to feel like a jet pilot who was losing engine power and was beginning a quick spiral straight downward. He felt rushed and hurried all of the time; he had to push himself to keep up with his competition, to stay on top. He began to spend less and less time with his wife and two children, had trouble sleeping at night, and suspected that he would soon develop ulcers just as his father did. He also told us that he had suspicions his wife might be cheating on him. His EMI score was in the high 400s. He and his wife sat down and talked about their life situation and decided that it would be a good idea for him to go through the EMM program—it was time for a change.

After going through the EMM 3-Day Crash Program, he was able to greatly reduce his feelings of "losing control," and his EMI score went down to the mid 200s. He told us that he had not exercised at all for the last two years, had begun to habitually neglect his diet, and had fallen into the habit of allowing himself only six hours of sleep each night, though he felt he probably needed seven to eight. He told us that after three days of exercise, eating properly, and allowing himself to get the sleep he needed, he felt physically better than he had in a long time. But what he thought was the most valuable part of the EMM program was taking the time to quietly sit down and take stock of his life, to reflect on what he really wanted out of life and how he really felt about the life he had begun to lead, to break the vicious cycle of rush-here-rush-there and to allow himself to plan a goal for his life, and a means of achieving that goal.

J.L. decided that what he really wanted out of life was to be successful at work, but also to have a happy family life. The EMM program allowed him to come to grips with the reality that he found no happiness in being the top man in his field if he experienced no joy in his life with his wife and children. Now his goal is to be a good businessman, but to place his family high on his list of priorities, even though it has meant a decrease in income. He found to his delight, that his family does not mind the decrease in income much—what they wanted was him, not his money. And he reports that he is happier than he has been in a long time.

G.M., female, secretary, 27. Approximately one year before she took part in the EMM program, she had been engaged to be married. A large wedding had been planned, with all her friends and relatives invited. The groom made a last-minute decision not to get married and moved out of the state without telling G.M., her family, or even his own family. G.M. had never been so deeply hurt or embarrassed in her life. Following that trauma, she experienced extreme anxiety when meeting men or going out on a date. After six months, her condition seemed to have gotten worse. She felt sad, alone, anxious about the prospect of being lonely for the rest of her life. When she first began the EMM program, her EMI score was around 400. After the 3-Day Crash Program it dropped to 300. After six months of the Lifelong Maintenance Program it fell below 200. After six months she reported that she was again able to meet men, to go out on dates and enjoy herself with much less anxiety than before. She said that the EMM program helped her get in touch with and understand her feelings of anxiety, and overcome the anxieties through the use of relaxation and imagery to desensitize her fear of men. She now believes that her future holds not loneliness and despair, but love and happiness.

P.F., male, 45, is a college professor in a small town on

the West Coast. His wife, S.P., also 45, is a housewife, and has not been employed since their marriage twenty years ago. Last year the last of their three sons got married and left home. They found themselves lonely and sad, without knowing why. Feeling the need for "something" in their lives, they took the EMM program together. At the beginning his EMI score was in the mid 300s, hers in the upper 300s. At the end of the 3-Day Crash Program they both brought their EMI scores down to the upper 200s. We interviewed them together, and they told us that the Crash Program allowed them to get in touch with their feelings and understand why they were experiencing a midlife "crisis." His crisis was the result of failing to reach the academic heights he had often dreamed about, and feeling that he was getting too old to ever do so. Hers resulted from living her life totally for her children, who were now gone. With these insights they were not so overwhelmed by their feelings, and felt much more able to rationally make decisions for their future.

Another of our subjects, V.T., female, 26 years of age, had found it necessary to quit her job because of her boss' illegal and unethical practices just before involving herself in the EMM program. She had held her job—head cashier for a department store—while she attended college. After graduation she got married and continued working as a cashier even though her interests lay in other fields, because she hadn't decided what direction her life should take. When she finally found it necessary to quit the cashiering job, she found herself faced with two major problems—the need for employment, and the need to decide what direction her life should take. She spent the first few weeks energetically seeking employment, but soon became depressed and frustrated after realizing she really did not know what kind of job she wanted, or even if she should go back to school for her Masters degree and only work part time. She felt tired, irritable, lacking energy, and defeated. Her depression started causing problems in her marriage. Her friends slowly began to fade away from her. She entered the EMM program.

At the beginning, her EMI score was in the mid 400s. After the 3-Day Crash Program, it dropped to the mid 300s. And after six months of the Lifelong Maintenance Program it dipped below 200. She reported that the EMM 3-Day Crash Program helped her break her self-defeating cycle of self-deprecation and depression by forcing her to discover what she wanted out of life. It helped her remember her talents, strengths, and all the things she really liked about herself, and to rationally work out a step-by-step program to achieve her goals. She is now back in school working toward her Masters degree in Special Education, and plans a career helping exceptional children. She reports that she, and her marriage, have never been better.

D.D., 52, male, was a devoted husband and a fine father to his six-year-old daughter. Last year, on her way home from school, his child was lured into a car by a strange man. She was found three days later face down in a nearby lake, dead. Six months later his wife told us that their little girl's death had ruined his life—he was now only a shell of a man. He was deeply depressed, could not sleep, lost a lot of weight, lost all interest in sex, and was experiencing difficulties at work. He refused to see a psychiatrist, but we convinced him to take part in the EMM program. At the start, his EMI score was dangerously high, in the low 500s. After the 3-Day Crash Program it was down to the low 400s. After six months of the Lifelong Maintenance Program, it was just slightly above 300. He has started to regain weight, his sexual appetite has returned, he sleeps better than he has in a long time, and he is regaining the respect of his boss. He later told us that he had allowed the grief caused by his daughter's senseless murder to cloud every part of his life until he could find no reason to live. The EMM program helped him to realize this, and to see beyond the feelings of grief, to get in touch with the things in life that were worth living for.

Of course we did not find that everybody in the EMM

group benefited significantly from the EMM program. There were a few that did not show large improvements in their feelings of anxiety, depression, or emotional stability. But a large majority did. Those that did not generally felt glad to have had the chance to experience the program and believed it would be useful sometime in their life.

And of course a few people dropped out of the program before it was finished. Nothing in life works for everybody all the time. And this certainly applies to the EMM program. In this day and age of fast-food restaurants and wonder drugs many people want to meet all their needs and solve all their problems quickly and with a minimum of effort. But conquering feelings of anxiety or depression, feelings of meaninglessness, or feelings that "things are not as good as they could be" can not be achieved instantly and passively. The EMM 3-Day Crash Program and the EMM Lifelong Maintenance Program are regimens that demand involvement and action by you. After interviewing several participants at length, we found that the more actively and totally you involve yourself in the program, the more benefit you will receive from it.

Bibliography

Adams, Ruth, and Murray, Frank. *Body, Mind and the B Vitamins.* New York: Larchmont Books, 1972.

Adler, Alfred. *The Practice and Theory of Individual Psychology.* New York: Humanities Press, Inc., 1971.

Aigner, H. "Health—Getting High On Ions." *New West* 17, August 1977.

Akiskal, H. S., and McKinney, W. T. "Depressive Disorders: Toward a Unified Hypothesis." *Science* (1973). 182:20.

Alexander, F.; Eisenstein, S.; and Grotjahn. M., editors. *Psychoanalytic Pioneers.* New York: Basic Books, 1966.

Alexander, G., and Selesnick, S. T. *The History of Psychiatry.* New York: New American Library, 1968.

Altschul, A. M. *Proteins: Their Chemistry and Politics.* New York: Basic Books, 1965.

Ayd, F. J., and Blackwell, B., editors. *Discoveries in Biological Psychiatry.* Philadelphia: J. B. Lippincott, 1970.

Bailey, Herbert. *Vitamin E: Your Key to a Healthy Heart.* New York: Arc Books, 1970.

Ban, T. A. *Psychopharmacology.* Baltimore: Williams and Wilkins, 1969.

Banik, N. L., and Davison, A. N. "Isolation of Purified Basic Protein from Human Brain." *Neurochemistry* (1973). 21:489.

Barbu, Z. *Problems of Historical Psychology*. New York: Grove Press, 1960.

Basowitz, H.; Persky, H.; Korchin, S. J.; and Grinker, R. R. *Anxiety and Stress*. New York: McGraw-Hill, 1955.

Basym, T. J. L. *About Mothers, Children and Their Nutrition*. London: Thorsons Publications, 1971.

Beck, A. T.; Ward, C. H.; Mendelson, M.; Mook, J.; and Erbarugh, J. "An Inventory for Measuring Depression." *Archives of General Psychiatry* (1961). 4:561.

Benjamin, Harry. *Your Diet in Health and Disease*. Croydon, Great Britain: Health for All Publications Company, 1931.

Bieler, Henry G. *Food is Your Best Medicine*. New York: Random House, 1965.

Bowerman, William J., and Harris, W. E. *Jogging*. New York: Grosset & Dunlap, 1967.

Bunney, W. E. Jr., and Davis, J. M. "Norepinephrine in Depressive Reactions." *Archives of General Psychiatry* (1965). 13:483.

Bunney, W. E. Jr.; Mason, J. W.; Roatch, J. F.; and Hamburg, D.A. "A Psychoendocrine Study of Severe Psychotic Depressive Crisis." *American Journal of Psychiatry* (1965). 122:72.

Chaney, Margaret S., and Ross, Margaret L. *Nutrition*. 8th ed. Boston: Houghton Mifflin Company, 1971.

Clarke, E., and Dewhurst, K. *An Illustrated History of Brain Function*. Berkeley: University of California Press, 1972.

Clausen, J. A., and Yarrow, M. R., editors. "The Impact of Mental Illness on the Family." *Journal of Social Issues* (1955). 11.

Coles, R. *Erik H. Erikson: The Growth of His Work*. Boston: Little, Brown, 1970.

Curtis, B. A.; Jacobson, S.; and Marcus, E. M. *An Introduction to the Neurosciences*. Philadelphia: Saunders, 1972.

Davis, J. M.; Janowsky, D. S.; and El-Yousef, M. K. "The Use of Lithium in Clinical Psychiatry." *Psychiatric Annual* (1973). 3:78.

Davis, K. E. *Drug Effects and Drug Use*. Monterey, California: Brooks/Cole Publishing Company, 1972.

De Becker. R. *The Understanding of Dreams and Their Influence on the History of Man*. New York: Hawthorn Books, 1968.

Deutsch, Albert. *The Mentally Ill in America*. New York: Columbia University Press, 1949.

Deutsch, Ronald M. *The Family Guide to Better Food and Better Health*. Des Moines, Iowa: Meredith Corporation, 1971.

Ehrman, L.; Omenn, G; and Caspari, E., editors. *Genetics, Environment and Behavior*. New York: Academic Press, 1972.

Erikson, Erik H. *Childhood and Society.* New York: W. W. Norton & Company, 1950.

Fieve, R. R. ed. "Depression in the 70's. Symposium." *Excerpta Medica,* Princeton, New Jersey, 1971.

Freedman, A. M.; Kaplan, H. I.; and Sadock, B. L. *Comprehensive Textbook of Psychiatry/I and II.* Vol. I. 2nd ed. Baltimore: Williams & Wilkins Company, 1975.

Freeman, W. *The Psychiatrist: Personalities and Patterns.* New York: Grune & Stratton, 1968.

Freud, S. "Inhibitions, Symptoms and Anxiety." *Standard Edition of the Complete Psychological Works of Sigmund Freud.* Vol. 20. London: Hogarth Press, 1959.

Good-hart, Robert S., and Shils, Maurice E. *Modern Nutrition in Health and Disease.* 5th ed. Philadelphia: Lea & Febiger, 1973.

Hale, N. G. *Freud and the Americans: The Beginnings of Psychoanalysis in the United States, 1876–1917.* New York: Oxford University Press, 1971.

Hall, Calvin S., and Lindzey, Gardner. *Theories of Personality.* New York: John Wiley & Sons, 1970.

Hebb, D. O. *A Textbook of Psychology.* 2nd ed. Philadelphia: W. B. Saunders, 1966.

Hendrick, I. *Facts and Theories of Psychoanalysis.* 3rd ed. New York: Alfred A. Knopf, 1958.

Holland, Morris K. *Psychology: An Introduction to Human Behavior.* Lexington, Massachusetts: D. C. Heath & Company, 1974.

Hill, D. "Depression: Disease, Reaction, or Posture?" *American Journal of Psychiatry* (1968). 125:445.

Hippocrates. *The Medical Works of Hippocrates.* Oxford: Blackwell, 1950.

Horney, K. *The Neurotic Personality of Our Time.* New York: W. W. Norton, 1937.

———. *Our Inner Conflicts: A Constructive Theory of Neurosis.* New York: W. W. Norton, 1945.

Howe, Phyllis S. *Basic Nutrition in Health and Disease.* 5th ed. Philadelphia: W. B. Saunders, 1971.

Jouvet, M. "Neurophysiology of the States of Sleep." *Physiology Review* (1967). 47:117.

Jung, Carl G. (Aniela Jaffe, ed.). *Memories, Dreams, Reflections.* New York: Pantheon Books, 1961.

Kety, S., and Schildkraut, J. J. "Biogenic Amines and Emotion." *Science* (1967). 156:21.

Klein, D. F., and David, J. M. *Diagnosis and Drug Treatment of Psychiatric Disorders.* Baltimore: Williams & Wilkins, 1969.

Lande, N. *Mindstyles/Lifestyles: A Comprehensive Overview of Today's Life-Changing Philosophies.* Los Angeles: Price/Stern/Sloan, 1976.

Lewin, K. A. *Dynamic Theory of Personality.* New York: McGraw-Hill, 1935.

Marx, J. L. "Biomedical Science: Immunology and Neurobiology to the Fore." *Science* (1973). 182:1329.

Masserman, J. *Behavior and Neurosis: An Experimental Psychoanalytic Approach to Psychobiologic Principles.* Chicago: University of Chicago Press, 1943.

Mathews, W. B., and Miller, H. *Diseases of the Nervous System.* Oxford: Blackwell, 1972.

Mendlewicz, J.; Fieve, R. R.; Rainer, J. D.; and Fleiss, J. L. "Manic Depressive Illness: A Comparative Study of Patients with and without a Family History." *British Journal of Psychiatry* (1972). 120:525.

Mikulas, W. L. *Behavior Modification: An Overview.* New York: Harper & Row, 1972.

Ostow, M. *Drugs in Psychoanalysis and Psychotherapy.* New York: Basic Books, 1962.

Pitts, F. N. Jr. "The Biochemistry of Anxiety." *Science Annual* (1969). 220: No. 2, p. 69.

Plutchik, R. "Emotions, Evaluation, and Adaptive Processes." *Feelings and Emotions.* New York: Academic Press, 1970.

Poe, R. O.; Lowell, F. M.; and Fox, H. M. "Depression Study of One Hundred Cases in a General Hospital." *Journal of the American Medical Association.* Medicine, 1966.

Pollitt, J. *Depression and Its Treatment.* London: Heinemann, 1965.

Rapaport, D. "Edward Bibring's Theory of Depression." *Collected Papers of David Rapaport.* M. Gill, ed. New York: Basic Books, 1967.

Rogers, C. R. *On Becoming a Person: A Therapist's View of Psychotherapy.* Boston: Houghton Mifflin, 1961.

————. *Becoming Partners: Marriage and Its Alternatives.* New York: Delacorte Press, 1972.

Sands, W. L. "Psychiatric History and Mental Status." *Comprehensive Textbook of Psychiatry.* A. M. Freedman and H. I. Kaplan, editors. Baltimore: Williams & Wilkins, 1967.

Sargant, William. *Battle for the Mind.* New York: Harper & Row, 1971.

Selye, H. *The Stress of Life.* New York: McGraw-Hill, 1956.

Shore, P. A.; Pletscher, A.; Tomich, E. G.; Carlsson, A.; Kuntzman, R.; and Brodie, B. B. "Role of Brain Serotonin in Reserpine Action." *Annual New York Academy of Science* (1957). 66:609.

Shore, P. A. "Release of Serotonin and Catecholamines by Drugs." *Pharmacological Review* (1962). 14:531.

Singer, I., and Rotenberg, D. "Mechanisms of Lithium Action." *New England Journal of Medicine* (1973). 289:254.

Skinner, B. F. "Some Contributions of an Experimental Analysis of Behavior to Psychology as a Whole." *American Psychology* (1953). 8:69.

Snyder, S. H. "New Developments in Brain Chemistry: Catecholamine Metabolism and its Relationship to the Mechanism of Action of Psychotropic Drugs." *American Journal of Orthopsychiatry* (1967). 7:864.

Spock, Benjamin. *Baby and Child Care.* New York: Simon and Schuster, 1973.

Stein, Z.; Susser, M.; Saenger, G.; and Marolla, F. "Nutrition and Mental Performance." *Science* (1972). 178.

Stenback, A. "Object Loss and Depression." *Archives of General Psychiatry* (1965). 12:144.

Stewart, W. A., and Freeman, L. *The Secret of Dreams.* New York: Macmillan, 1972.

Sullivan. H. S. *The Interpersonal Theory of Psychology.* New York: W. W. Norton, 1953.

Szasz, T. *The Myth of Mental Illness.* New York: Harper and Row, 1964.

Thompson, K. C., and Hendrie H. C. "Environmental Stress in Primary Depressive Illness." *Archives of General Psychiatry* (1972). 26:130.

Truex, R. C., and Carpenter, M. B. *Human Neuroanatomy.* Baltimore: Williams & Wilkins, 1969.

Walsh, E. G. *Physiology of the Nervous System.* London: Longmans, 1964.

Watson, John B. *Behaviorism.* New York: W. W. Norton. 1970.

Weiner, N., and Rabidjija, M. "The Regulation of Norepinephrine Synthesis. Effect of Puromycin on the Accelerated Synthesis of Norepinephrine Associated with Nerve Stimulation." *Journal of Pharmacology and Experimental Therapeutics* (1968). 164:103–104.

Weiss, J. M. "Effects of Coping Responses on Stress." *Journal of Comparative Physiological Psychology* (1968). 65:251.

Whybrown, P., and Parlatore, A. "Melancholia, a Model in Madness: A Discussion of Recent Psychobiologic Research into Depressive Illness." *Psychiatry* (1973). 4:351.

Williams, T. A.; Katz, M. M.; and Shield, J. A. Jr., editors. "Recent Advances in the Psychobiology of Depressive Illness." *Proceedings of a Workshop Sponsored by the National Institute of Mental Health, Department of Health Education and Welfare Publication No. 70–9053.* Washington: United States Government Printing Office, 1972.

Wolf, S., and Goodell. H. *Stress and Disease.* 2nd ed. Springfield, Illinois: Thomas, 1968.

Wolpe, J. "The Experimental Foundations of Some New Psychotherapeutic Methods." *Experimental Foundations of Clinical Psychology.* A. J. Bachrach, ed. New York: Basic Books, 1962.

Wooldridge, Dean E. *The Machinery of the Brain.* New York: McGraw-Hill, 1963.

Zung. W. W. K. "Evaluating Treatment Methods for Depressive Disorders." *American Journal of Psychiatry* (1968). 124: Supplement 40.

INDEX

abdominal exercises, 116–17
acceptance (unconditional), and
    creativity, 211
acetylcholine
    and memory, 138
    and tardive dyskinesia, 137
achievement, and parental expec-
    tations, 152–53
adrenaline, and neurotransmitters, 8
affirmation cards, 36
    use of, 50–51, 65, 75, 84, 94
aggression, and blood pressure, 20
air quality, and emotional health,
    45–46
Alcmaeon of Croton, 70
amines, and depression, 8
amino acids, and proteins, 123–24
anxiety
    and control, 21
    and depression, 201
    and dread, 204–205
    and psychological stress, 191
    and tension, 187
Arabic cultures, in Middle Ages, 72
Aristotle, 70, 71
arm exercises, 117–19
ascorbic acid. *See* Vitamin C
Augustine, Saint, 71

Bannister, Roger, 111
B-complex vitamins, 38, 127–28,
    193
Beck, Aaron, 200
Bettelheim, Bruno, 21
bicycling, benefits of, 110

"biogenic amine hypothesis" (of
    depression), 72–73
blood pressure, and aggression, 20
body, and mind, 69–74, 217
brain
    and depression, 7–8, 73–74
    and diet, 136–38
    and sleep, 34n, 35n
    see also serotonin
Breen, Dr. Warren, 4
brewer's yeast, value of, 131
Brown, Robert S., 37n
Bunney, Dr. William E., Jr., 198

Cannon, Walter, 21
carbohydrates, and brain, 34n, 35n
caring, importance of, 84
cereals, value of, 126
change, 146
    and identity, 156–57
    and roles, 160–61
chemicals (body)
    and depression, 7–8
    and mental illness, 72–74
    and sleep, 34n, 35n
    see also serotonin, tryptophan
China (ancient), philosophy in, 69
choice-making, need for, 112
choline, value of, 128, 137–38
circulatory exercises, 119–21
co-enzymes, and vitamins, 124
communication, and relationships,
    168–71, 175–76
competence, and emotional growth,
    164–65

235